# PRAISE FOR A PLACE THEY LOVE

*A Place They Love* is a great read for new teachers, and a great reminder for those of us that have been teaching for a long time!

JESSICA LACOUR, DEAN OF ACADEMICS

Who doesn't want a pristine place to learn and grow? In this book, Elijah does what NO other author in education does: He confronts the type of schools students should reside in and he outlines spaces where both students and teachers can learn and grow together. This book is a motivational diamond and a place where education is celebrated and appreciated! Use it with your staff. Use it with your students. Read it alone. Learn and grow. Epic adventure!

DR. RICK JETTER, AUTHOR / CO-FOUNDER OF PUSHING BOUNDARIES CONSULTING, LLC

This book is great for the new teacher, the exhausted teacher, the teacher trying to remember their why, and for anyone who wants to help shape and ignite a new normal. Elijah takes us on a journey through his career and evolution as an educator, allowing each of us the opportunity to look back to move ahead.

DR. DAVE SCHMITTOU, AUTHOR / DIRECTOR OF LEADERSHIP AND DEVELOPMENT WITH THE TEACH BETTER TEAM

Elijah takes you on a journey through his own lived experiences, successes, failures, lessons learned, and positive butterfly effect that engaging with the education community at large can have on your development as an educator. Colleagues and former students even chime in within the pages showing you how one educator can make an incredible difference in the lives of other human beings; just imagine what 100, 1,000, or 10,000 effective educators can do? Give yourself the gift of a new perspective with Elijah's book and see what nuggets of wisdom you can use in your classroom today!

BECKY SCHNEKSER, NATIONAL GEOGRAPHIC
CERTIFIED EDUCATOR / EXPLORER / AUTHOR
OF *EXPEDITION SCIENCE: EMPOWERING
LEARNERS THROUGH EXPLORATION*

A heartfelt, honest commentary from a dedicated teacher who clearly strives to serve his children. This book is a must read for any educator looking to build a space that their students will love.

CHARLES WILLIAMS, PRINCIPAL / CO-AUTHOR
OF *INSIDE THE PRINCIPAL'S OFFICE: A
LEADERSHIP GUIDE TO INSPIRE REFLECTION
AND GROWTH*

# A PLACE THEY LOVE

## CREATING A HEALTHY SCHOOL CULTURE AND POSITIVELY IMPACTING STUDENTS

### ELIJAH CARBAJAL

EduMatch
PUBLISHING

ISBN: 978-1-959347-06-4

*For the teachers in my family, especially my late Grandpa Barney Carbajal Jr. (the original Mr. C.) and my mom, Theresa Carbajal. Thank you for paving the way for me.*

*For the mentor teachers in my life — Tracey Taylor, Heidi Dudley, and Adrienne Jaramillo. You've helped to shape me into the educator that I am today. Thank you.*

*For all the educators reading this book, striving to make school a place that students love. Let's walk this path together.*

# CONTENTS

# INTRODUCTION: FIRST STEPS

It's so exciting to see a child take their first steps. I have no children of my own, but I have nieces and nephews. To see them go from crawling to walking is exciting. Firsts are always exciting. First words, first haircut, first tooth, first *pulled* tooth, first boyfriend/girlfriend, first kiss. Firsts rock!

Storytime!

My first time stepping into a classroom was very exciting and nerve-wracking. You see, I was homeschooled by my mom, K-12. My mom, Theresa, was a former special education teacher in Belen, NM, for about six years before she and my dad decided to start a family. I had never been to a school, or at least not a classroom. That's right: *my first time stepping into a public school classroom was my first day of student teaching!*

You might be wondering, why would a homeschooled kid who lived (sort of) in the middle of nowhere, with absolutely no knowledge of anything related to public school want to become a public school teacher?! It is odd that I went into education, and at the same time, not really. I come from a family of service, mostly in the military. My dad, Rick, served 32 years in the United States Air Force. My brother, Ricky, was a United States Marine. My brothers, Jonah and Michael, are United States Airmen. My brother, Stephen, is a firefighter, and my sister, Francesca (lovingly referred to as Frankie), is a caregiver for her husband's aunt. Both my grandpas were war veterans (Grandpa Barney in World War II and Papa Edenio in Korea). My dad and Ricky were actually in Iraq (different locations) at the same time. Ricky also served in Afghanistan. When it was getting close to my high school graduation (I got my GED, y'all!), I was asked by several of my family members, friends, and close peers if I was planning to enlist in a branch of the military. I told them that I had thought about it, and as odd as it seemed, I had decided not to enlist in the military. See, since I was 14 years old, I knew I was going to follow a different set of family footprints.

You see, Grandpa Barney became a teacher after serving as a First Generation Airmen. My grandma Olga was also a school teacher. They both taught different subjects, including music. My dad's brother, my Uncle Barney, became a band director, and a darn good one from what I hear. My late Aunt Roberta "Bobbie" Carbajal was my piano teacher. As I mentioned, my mom was a special education teacher. I became inspired by the stories I heard about my grandpa, how no student or teacher would cross him. Not because he was a jerk, but because he was respected. I liked hearing how my uncle could get a bunch of squirrelly high schoolers to perform with excellence. And being around my mom and aunt were some of the most peaceful and loving moments of my childhood.

As I said, I decided to walk the other family path: *teaching.*

Initially, I wanted to be...any guesses? If you guessed a Toys R Us Kid, you're a little off. If you guessed music teacher, you are absolutely correct! (If I could give you a high five through this book, I would!) I learned everything about music I could. I didn't really know how to prepare for teaching. I watched my mom teach, but that was with six kids in the comfort of her home. I guess my learning would come with my college studies and student teaching.

Eventually, I was talked into switching programs from music education to general education by my college advisor. "There is always a need for elementary and middle school teachers, especially male teachers," they told me. Well, as long as I got to teach, I was all for it. Eventually, I graduated in December 2014 with a Bachelor's Degree in Elementary Education and received my K-8 license with an endorsement in social studies.

But let's back up a bit. Let's back up to the day I started student teaching. Let's focus on the entire iceberg, not just the tip of it.

Walking in and greeting Mrs. Jaramillo was exciting. Seeing a room full of 22 sixth graders was intimidating. Some of them were almost as tall as me (I'm only 5'9"). I was excited to start learning how to teach. I was put in charge of teaching science when I was there, and even had the experience of teaching an entire day when my mentor teacher's substitute didn't show up. It was pretty cool. That was the first time that I felt like I could run a classroom. Things were about to change.

The following year, I finished up my student teaching at a school in Albuquerque, NM. This time it was fourth grade. (The students were much shorter than me now.) Around early October, the principal offered to let me take over the class I was student teaching in and move my mentor teacher over to another classroom. I officially took the job in November. It was my first "big boy" job! Boy, was I excited! I was such a greenhorn, but the excitement was there. I was able to run a classroom the way I wanted, and teach kids things I was passionate about. I was excited to grow and develop as a teacher. The excitement, however, didn't last very long.

The class I taught was very tough. I had behavior issues with several students. I realized very quickly that I didn't know how to manage a classroom and deal with conflict. I also realized I didn't know how to teach. There was content (yes, fourth-grade content) that I found myself very confused about at first. And then the paperwork. Oh, my goodness. I found myself drowning in paperwork. I was also stumbling over the papers and tests that needed to be graded, the homework that wasn't getting turned in, and the other requirements that come with teaching: IEP meetings, PLC meetings, keeping data logs, state testing, formal observations, parent/teacher conferences...the list goes on and on.

By the end of the year, I was so excited and just happy that I survived. I'm not sure how, but I did, and so did my students. Some of my students were even sad that the year was over. I packed up my classroom and took my personal belongings with me. Because I started in the middle of the year, the district wasn't required to offer me a job next year. And I was actually relieved. I didn't want to go back into the classroom. Yeah, that's right. I was done.

My college professors told me that if you could make it past year three, then you were really meant to teach. (Horrible advice, by the way.) Well, I barely survived year one, and I was over it. My first steps were hardly steps. I fell and got lots of bumps and bruises along the way. I decided it was time to get the heck out of dodge and find another career.

The job search didn't go well. I found myself believing the (not true) statement that those who can't work should teach. I realized I was trained to teach, or at least had been training to teach, not to do anything else I applied for. So, when the call came from the school where I had just taught, asking me to return and teach fourth grade again, I was a little relieved and scared at the same time. I hadn't learned to walk like a teacher yet. I was afraid of falling and getting bruised all over again. I only took the job because I needed money to survive.

What I found out the next year was that I *had* learned to walk. I found myself keeping up with grading tests and other work. I was collaborating with other teachers. I was building relationships with students, and my classroom management was much better than the year before. I wasn't falling down as much. I still had to strengthen my legs and my balance, but I could stand, and I could walk.

**Stop and reflect: What first steps have you taken in your life? In your teaching career?**

The first steps are exciting, intimidating, difficult, and promising. Not just the first steps for children—the symbolic first steps in our careers. The first steps as a married couple or as a parent. The first step in the classroom as a teacher or as a student in a new grade level.

I teach students to take the first steps. They may push back a bit, scared to fall, but eventually, they learn to walk all on their own. That math concept that was so daunting now is aced! Those big vocabulary words that they could barely pronounce are now being used in discussions or in writing. First steps towards solving problems with other peers. The first steps to creating art they have no idea that they are capable of creating. The first steps to helping them discover their passions and lifelong dreams. Throughout the book, we will look at ways that we can encourage students to take those first steps.

As teachers, we encourage students to take risks and try new things.

We want to see them grow and develop. They shape themselves and grow into who they are by taking the first steps we motivate and teach them to take. This means that we are at the forefront. Students need to see us take the first steps. They'll find courage from us when they see us courageously take our own first steps.

The first steps are taken very early on. For me, it was actually going to college and pursuing a degree in education. Only we don't stop taking our first steps there. Remember, I hadn't stepped foot into an actual public school classroom until I started student teaching. The first year of teaching was definitely a big first step. As we continue through our careers of teaching, we realize that there are other first steps we must take. Perhaps it's going back to college for a master's degree, moving into a leadership role, switching grade levels, or switching to a different position of teaching.

One of the other first steps I had to take was breaking away from traditional styles of assessments and instruction. I had moved to Aztec, NM, after my third year of teaching and was now teaching at a fourth- and fifth-grade school. It was during my fifth year of teaching that my assistant principal recommended reading *Kids Deserve It* by Adam Welcome and Todd Nesloney. That book changed the way I teach for good! While reading the book, I began to push myself to take steps toward more engaging lessons. That year was definitely a big year for me. I took my first steps, stumbled a bit, got a few bumps, but eventually was walking with confidence. That year was different. I taught biography by dressing as Blackbeard and making the students the "hostages" on *Queen Ann's Revenge*. My students got to hear from "Blackbeard" himself, unlock cell doors that they were "trapped" in, and even stole the treasure—Pirate Booty, Hugs Juice, and Chips Ahoy! Cookies—from Blackbeard's treasure chest. I taught theme and point of view through song lyrics, dressing as John Lennon, and playing and singing Beatles music. I transformed my class into a cafe, a campground, a graveyard, a football field, and outer space—all the first steps that my students got to see me take.

*I got out of their way because I believed in them.*

*Kids Deserve It* also inspired me to push my students towards their first steps. The authors Adam Welcome and Todd Nesloney (2016) say, "Far too often, our students aren't the ones who limit themselves. We do...We must believe in our kids—empower them. We must be in the business of removing boundaries for kids..." (pp. 96-97). Those words made me check to see if I was really holding my kids back, and it challenged me to remove boundaries, not to create new ones. So I began letting my students lead the discussions instead of merely participating in a pre-planned discussion. I began letting them teach the class. I got out of their way because I believed in them to take their first steps.

One kiddo, in particular, comes to mind. She was very much what I consider a student who was inside the box. She was good at school but didn't really do much exploring. She wasn't a risk-taker. I continued to challenge her to expand her thinking, try new things, and take risks. By the end of the year, she was writing beautiful poetry. She was expanding her thinking, even volunteering to teach the class new concepts. She grew so much. I'm proud of who she became and the steps she took to better herself. She didn't just peek outside the box; she destroyed that box! She really left an impact on my life. (Look for her contribution in the chapter "Sorry, Fun Friday's Over.")

**Stop and reflect: What first steps have you seen your students take? How did you support them as they learned to "walk"?**

That's what school should be like—a place where students learn to take their first steps. That means we need to be there for them. Be there to support them when they take risks, encourage them when they fall, and celebrate with them when they are successful. That, to me, sounds like a place where students love to be.

Teachers, this book is for you. Whether you are in need of encouragement to leave behind outdated practices or to continue doing the amazing things you are doing. In this book, we're going to look at ways that we can contribute to making our schools and our classrooms a place where students love to be. It's going to challenge you to take risks, try new things, and work towards mastering the science and art of teaching. You will be encouraged to join me as we work to break from outdated educational norms and styles of teaching. You will be encouraged to do what you can to make education fun, engaging, and safe.

Administrators, this book is speaking primarily to teachers, but don't worry; there is a chapter I wrote just for you. In that chapter, you will be encouraged to continue doing what is best for students and teachers and (if needed) encourage you to stop any practices that don't promote a positive school culture.

In this book, you'll find different ideas for how you can help students take their first steps, as well as how you can take some new first steps of your own. Are you ready? Let's do this. Take the first step.

# CHAPTER 1
# *READY. SET. BRING IT!*

T eachers have one of the most important jobs in the world. I might be a little biased, yes, but roll with me. Think for a minute about all that teachers do.

## THE MANY HATS A TEACHER WEARS.

We teach academic content (reading, writing, math, science, social studies, and more). That's obvious, I know. Stop for a second, though, and think about the gravity of that. We are responsible for teaching students for an entire school year. We need to pass along knowledge and wisdom that they will carry forever. We have the potential to be the best or the worst teacher they may have, depending on how well we teach the content and connect with the students and their families. That's an immense pressure that terrifies me. I am pretty confident in myself to get the job done; however, there's always some uncertainty. What if I'm not successful at reaching every student? What if I can't get through to some students? What if... August Burns Red has a song titled "Invisible Enemy." I can't help but think about those screaming lyrics, "Beliefs set aside, the uncertainty is what's truly terrifying!" I'm reminded of just how true that is for me as an educator.

We serve our students and their families by providing the best education possible. We serve our students by providing experiences, interventions, supports, and strategies for their needs. We serve them, sometimes by giving them the things that they may not have, such as snacks, warm clothes, or school supplies.

We teach social skills. While a great deal of this responsibility falls on families, we are with these kiddos for six hours a day for over nine months. We impact them greatly. We model and teach them how to behave, solve problems, maintain friendships, and work hard.

We are role models for students. As a male teacher, I'm reminded of this over and over again and then some more: *I wanted my child in your class because they need a positive male role model in their life.* (I wish I had a dollar for every time I heard that phrase.) The pressure is on me to be that positive role model every day; what I say and do impacts my kids every day. Regardless of your gender, the same is true for you. Your words and actions are being closely analyzed by your students. They are learning from you even when you don't think that they are.

We teach them social/emotional skills. I don't spill all of the gory details about my struggles, but I am pretty honest with my students, telling them that I have depression and anxiety. I am open with how I handle my emotions. I love to use literature as a way of teaching kids all sorts of strategies for dealing with a wide range of emotions.

## Students are learning from you, even when you don't think that they are.

We are C-H-E-E-R Leaders! We cheer students from the bleachers at football games. We applaud them for their efforts in dance. We congratulate them for a job well done after showing their livestock at the county fairs.

There's probably a list of things that you do for your students with responsibilities I didn't mention. The point of all this is to say that we have a huge role to play in their lives. Because we play such an important role in their lives, we need to be on our A-game daily. We need to be ready to bring it to them. Bringing our best to our classrooms is what will make school a place where they love to be.

## BRING THE EXPERIENCES.

It's time to bring them experiences that will spark their creativity, inspire them to chase their dreams and work hard to be successful. Don't settle for being a good teacher when your students deserve an excellent teacher. This may mean that you have to do things differently than how you are doing them now. That's scary, I know. The unknown always is, but when you change for the better, remember who you are directly impacting: the kids. When you bring it to them—your energy, passion, excitement, engagement, encouragement, and compassion—your students will be grateful.

When I teach themes and points of view to my class, I use music and lyrics instead of textbook poetry. The kids connect to music way more than a textbook. I have gotten some, well, interesting looks from teachers when I dress up as people like John Lennon, decked with a long-haired wig, or when I dress as Skillet front man, John Cooper, with full eyeliner. I don't care, though, that I am doing things differently than other teachers because, in the end, I'm getting different results. Besides, I'm not bringing it for other teachers. I don't care what anyone else on my campus thinks about my pedagogy and my methods. I'm doing it for my kids. I'm bringing it for them!

**Stop and reflect: How do you bring your passion, excitement, and engagement to the classroom daily?**

## BRING POSITIVITY.

Bring your positivity to the classroom as well. Don't bring that negativity in with you. Don't be that teacher who complains to their kids. Don't be the grumpy teacher. Your kids feed off of your attitude and energy, whether that attitude and energy are good or bad. Bring a positive attitude, a calm spirit, and an energetic vibe. You'll notice an immediate difference in the atmosphere when you bring the positive and leave behind the negative. Your kids will also notice it. More on this in the chapter, "Shut Up and Teach," but for now, here are some tips on how to leave your negative behind.

- Journaling. I find that writing out my negative feelings helps me from projecting them verbally. Writing my thoughts, even negative thoughts, helps keep them out of my head.
- Listen to your music. I didn't say calm, classical, or instrumental music. Listen to music that relaxes *you*. (Full disclosure: I'm the teacher who pulls up to school bumpin' punk rock, metal, or rap music.) If it relaxes you, motivates you, or makes you smile, crank up the volume on that!
- Work it out. Walking, running, or any physical exercise is, obviously, good for our bodies, but it also allows us to stress ourselves positively while releasing some of that negativity that may be clouding our minds.
- Change your routine for the day. Do you normally get coffee from the teacher's lounge? On your way to work, treat yourself to a coffee from your favorite coffee shop. Sometimes I would change the route I took to work, or even the route to walk to the front office when I got to school. Changes like that can give us new eyes to see things we don't normally don't, while practicing a healthy avoidance of some of the things that may be stressing us out.

## BRING YOUR MISTAKES.

Yeah, your mistakes. Teaching through your mistakes is extremely powerful. I've made my fair share of mistakes, some extremely embarrassing. I had to apologize for losing my temper, for wrongly accusing students, and for not being more prepared. I don't always bring my A-game when I should. I am human, after all, and so are you. You will have days when you mess up. Don't be too proud to apologize for those mistakes. This teaches students that it is okay to make a mistake. It also teaches them that you care enough about your students to make amends when you fall short. You're building better relationships with your students and making a big impact. (More on this in the chapter "The Importance of Failing.")

**Stop and reflect: What mistakes have you made as a teacher? How did you make it right with your students?**

———————

Now is the time to bring it to our kids. Remember, it's about making school a place where students love to be. We make it that place by bringing our A-game to school and apologizing for the shortcomings of our B-game. We make it that place by being excited about and engaged in the work we do in the classroom. We make school a place they love to be by showing up every day, ready to teach, inspire, and learn with our students.

## CHAPTER 2
# THE UNKNOWN

So you've decided that the time to take your first steps is now. You have the "Ready. Set. Bring It!" mindset. The next step is into the unknown.

Storytime!

I had the fantastic opportunity to free swim with sharks in Hawaii. About three miles out from the beach is a spot where the ocean currents merge, allowing sharks to coast after they have fed for most of the night—kind of a chill time for sharks. It's amazing.

Was I scared? Well, yeah, a little. I'm not a great swimmer in a pool, let alone in the open ocean, three miles from the beach. The wind was rather severe that day, which made the boat really "bouncy"; I wasn't sure how I was supposed to swim in the water. Plus, when you get into the ocean, you kind of become subject to whatever is in there. I had no idea what kind of sharks we would see or if we would see any other marine life. There was a little element of uncertainty. Uncertainty brings fear or at least nervousness.

I was nervous as the boat came to a stop. Looking over the edge of the boat, I could see shark fins (yeah, just like in the movies). Sharks circling the boat, just waiting for us to jump in, kind of made me nervous. But there was no backing down. I knew I had to do this!

Then came the moment when my feet hit the water. At that moment, I had a thought: *Is this the dumbest thing I've ever done?* Another thought came as my head went underwater and I saw the first shark: *This is one of the coolest things I've ever done!*

As I was swimming, taking in the beauty of the open ocean, these magnificent creatures were swimming all around me. The largest, a female Galapagos shark about 11 feet in length, eyed me at the surface of the water. She was beautiful! She moved through the water with ease and grace. We had an understanding. Neither of us was there to harm the other. After a short while, I looked straight down. Counting over 20 sharks, I saw that each was moving freely. As far as I could see, until the water of the ocean faded to black, there were sharks. I asked about this. "There have to be more sharks, bigger sharks, deep in the black, right?" I was told by our guide that, yes, there is even the potential for great whites and mako sharks to be well beneath us.

So. Freaking. Cool.

## LESSONS FROM THE SHARKS.

I learned a lot that day about sharks, but I also learned about diving (pun) into the unknown. We are teachers. We have the task of teaching new content to students for the first time. We have the opportunity to challenge them. We have the privilege of encouraging our students to take risks. We are leaders. We are the ones who should be leading our kids into the unknown.

*You can't let fear of the unknown keep you from diving in and taking on something new.*

The unknown can be scary for lots of reasons. Heading into unknown territory is risky. We can anticipate but can't predict what kind of challenges will arise. We don't know how well or not something will go over when trying something new. *What if I try that new thing and it doesn't pan out the way I thought it would? What if my students are confused even more when I try this in class?* That's why a lot of teachers don't venture out into the unknown. The "What if" teachers will always play it safe. Not that having those questions is bad—it's good to think about all the possible outcomes, and making a plan for those moments, but you can't let fear of the unknown keep you from diving in and taking on something new.

## YOU SHOULD JUMP IN.

The unknown can paralyze us if we allow it. As educators, we need to be the ones to jump in with the sharks. We take risks, and they pay off...or they don't, but that's okay as long as we learn from them. The most important thing is that we are taking risks, that we are not hanging on to the side of the boat, paralyzed by the fear of failing or fear of the unknown. The pure joy of swimming with the sharks only happens if we get in the water. The success and reward of trying something new will only come if we actually try something new. Take a risk. Take the first step. Then the next. Then another. Keep trying new things. Your kids will appreciate it.

**Stop and reflect: What lessons have you learned from facing the unknown and diving in?**

Your kids will also be inspired by it. See, kids try things that their parents, teachers, and peers do. When you make stepping out into the unknown okay and safe, they will find the courage to do the same. For some, this may mean that they try out for sports, the drama team, the debate team, and more. For students learning to read, it means trying to read a book just above their current reading level. It may mean conducting experiments that challenge the way we think. For older students, it might mean applying to colleges, filling out scholarship applications, or getting a tutor to help bring a low grade up. Whatever it is, our students will rise to the occasion as we challenge them to take risks and step into the unknown.

*The success and reward of trying something new only comes if we actually try something new.*

## LEAD WITH YOUR ACTIONS.

We set an example for our kids. They need to see us try something new, even if we don't have all of the answers. During the year that I am writing this, I tried something new with my class called The Grid Method. The Grid Method was created by Chad Ostrowski, M.S. Ed—Co-Author of *Teach Better* (2019)/CEO - Teach Better Team (@chadostrowski). The Grid Method is "...a student-centered, competency-based framework, created at the classroom level and designed to fit any teacher's style, within any curriculum, in any classroom" (Teach Better: The Grid Method, 2021). The Grid Method is designed to give more control to students to work at their own pace until full mastery of a skill is accomplished. I wasn't sure how things were going to go with my class. This class had some students who had difficulty regulating their behavior and had a hard time staying organized. They relied a lot on my support or support from others, so switching to mastery learning was going to be a shock to them. I still gave them support, I still taught, and I helped when they needed it. But I was nervous about how much ownership the kids would take. I believed 100% in the Grid Method, and I was committed to trying it. Even if it took weeks to get into a groove of learning with this new approach, I was going to dive into it.

What's funny is that the same feeling I had when my feet hit the cold ocean water was present the day I introduced my class to the Grid Method. What if this is a total flop? What if my kids can't handle it? What if I didn't set it up correctly? So many thoughts flooded my mind that it was literally making me sick. (Damn that anxiety, right?) But just like there was no turning back when I hit the water, the day was here. I was in it!

I introduced it to the kids. There was no fighting or arguing when I told them that they had to pass with 80% to move forward. There was a little bit of a learning curve. I had to adjust to teaching different levels, different lessons, and skills, all within 90 minutes. I had to figure out which mini-lessons were going to be the most beneficial. But it was okay. The kids were learning. They were showing growth, moving through the grid, and they were enjoying the work they were doing.

After a few weeks, I was wondering how they would do on their quarterly exams. The results were similar to that feeling I had when my head went underwater and saw the first shark. I was happy that I stepped into the unknown because my data looked good. Not great. I still had some struggling students, but the average student score on the math assessment jumped up by 12%, and the percentage of kids proficient increased by 5%. For reading, I was able to identify areas where each student struggled, which would help me differentiate the instruction when we moved forward.

## A WORLD IN CHAOS.

When the world was thrown into chaos due to the COVID-19 outbreak, all across the world, countries were placed on lockdown. Bars, malls, movie theaters, and other public venues were closed for...well, no one quite knew. Schools across America were ordered to shut down for the remainder of the year and switch to virtual learning.

That was unknown territory. It provided a great opportunity for teachers to grow. It was a great chance for teachers to show students that while the situation we found ourselves in sucked and was very unfortunate, we could still dive in to swim with the sharks. We could still be brave and tackle any new challenge and conquer it as well. (More on this in the chapter "Dear Administration.")

## FUN IS PART OF THE EXPERIENCE.

Educators, while you are braving the unknown, conquering your fears, and overcoming your doubt, remember to have fun! Remember that we are trying to make school a place that kids love to be at. Swimming with sharks was a blast! Would I do it again? Abso-freakin-lutely! It was so much fun, and I'm glad I got that experience. You'll find that when you step into the unknown, you will enjoy it, as long as you have the right perspective. If you are in it to make school fun, challenging, and enjoyable, then the unknown will present so many positive takeaways. You'll find learning opportunities, discover areas that need improvement, and develop new strengths. The same is true for our students who step out. They will learn to love the process and enjoy the challenges that come. They will learn a lot about themselves and make memories that will last for a long time.

**Stop and reflect: Who can you go to for support when facing the unknown?**

---

Challenges, especially the ones we learn from, make school fun! The unknown presents opportunities to learn. I never knew sharks were docile until I jumped into the water. We will never know just how fun school can be until we step out and try something new. We won't know what our students or we are capable of until we challenge ourselves and step out. It's scary but rewarding. It's uncertain but worth the risk.

Are you ready to swim with the sharks? It's time.

# CHAPTER 3
# *THE ENGAGED TEACHER*

It was one of those days. I was trying my hardest to keep my kids under control and quiet. That should've been a dead giveaway that the problem was NOT the students. I couldn't understand why my class was so riled up. It was like they were being pumped with sugar all day.

I had maxed out on the day. I had about all I could take. So by the time the kids left, I was exhausted and ready to complain. I spoke and listened to fellow teachers complain about the same things—day one of state testing, no extra recesses, full moon last night, the kids had just gotten back from spring break. Embarrassingly, I admit that I joined in with them. My kids' energy levels were low. They weren't engaged at all. They...

And that's when the thought hit me: *Maybe I wasn't engaged. Maybe my energy levels were low.*

You know that saying that an engaged student isn't a behavior problem? Sadly, I used to use that idea to pin a student down.

*Well, if she would just engage herself...*

*If he was more engaged in the lesson...*

What would happen if we stopped writing the narrative for students and focused on our story? What would happen if we looked inward first instead of pointing the blame on our students? What results would occur if we, through mindful reflection, restructured our lessons to be more engaging and brought our A-game instead of settling for our B-game?

**Stop and reflect: What does an engaged teacher look like to you? Can you describe them in a couple of sentences?**

## AS MUCH AS THE LESSON ALLOWS.

The problem that day wasn't that my students weren't engaged. They were. They were engaged *as much as the lesson allowed them to be.* The bigger issue was that my lesson wasn't inviting them to engage on another level. Furthermore, I wasn't excited. I wasn't teaching with the excitement and energy that I normally taught with. So, naturally, my students matched my energy level. Always remember, most of your students will meet you where you are at. Nine times out of 10, they feed off of the energy you bring into the room.

If we plan to make school a place that students love to be at, then we need to teach like it's a place that we love to be at. I understand that there will be days when we don't feel like being at our jobs. We're human, and we experience days where it seems that it would be easier to call a sub so we could stay in bed a little longer, get caught up on the mountain of laundry, or just rest up. To say that we would rather be elsewhere on some days is normal.

If you can't bring your best to kids daily, and if you find yourself constantly wishing to be somewhere else, then it may be time to start evaluating why. Burnout is real, and teacher stress is totally a thing. The sad part is that they are becoming more prevalent, especially since the COVID-19 pandemic hit the world. Madeline Will cites a survey in *EdWeek* that states, "More than a quarter of teachers said job-related stress leads them to think often about quitting, and 16 percent said they dread going to work every day" (Will, *Teachers Are Not OK, Even Though We Need Them to Be,* 2021). Furthermore, she claims that "...42 percent of teachers said administrators have not made any efforts to help relieve their stress" (2021). More must be done to fix the system that is making teacher burnout normality. I don't have all the answers, but I can say this: if nothing changes, nothing changes. If (borrowing the title of the previous article mentioned) the teachers are not okay, even though we need them to be, maybe we should start asking questions. Questions like:

- Why is teacher burnout expected normality of a teacher's career?
- Beside the cliche "Make sure that you practice self-care" speech, what is actually being done to promote the mental wellness of educators on a large scale?
- How do we expect educators to prioritize their mental health if more and more is added to their plate without removing anything from the plate? (Remember, teachers don't need bigger plates. Sometimes, they need an item or two removed from the plate.)

All the self-care practices you can practice can't fix a broken system, an extremely large class size, lack of prep-time, staff shortages, lack of support from leadership, or any of the other factors contributing to teacher stress and burnout. Teachers' self-care practices should be a part of daily life, not a "pull in case of emergency" type of thing.

Now, teachers, there are some things that you *can do* for yourself. In a recent *Edutopia* article, Dr. Kevin Leichtman (author of *The Perfect Ten*) gives some important strategies for teachers dealing with burnout. He encourages teachers to practice self-care through outlets like exercise, meditation, or counseling, to build up self-efficacy by taking pride in our abilities, and to find a mentor who will help you, not complain with you, during the hard times (Leichtman, *How to Fight Burnout*, 2021). I can testify about that last part. Mentors or teacher partners at school, not on Twitter, are often the ones who help me in my low moments by reminding me that I'm not alone, and that I have help and support right across the hall from my classroom.

If you find that you are struggling to engage yourself and bring passion into the classroom, then perhaps it's time to consider a change in position, school, or even career. There's nothing wrong with that, by the way. Some educators will realize that they don't find joy and reward in teaching students. Some only find it within certain ages and grades. Then there are the educators who have found their calling in equally important roles in education: instructional coaches, principals, interventionists, curriculum instructors, etc. All those positions are important, and if that's where you find your passion, then go for it.

## IMMERSED IN LEARNING.

If you're going to be in the classroom, you have to be immersed in the learning with your students. You are the one who is meant to inspire and excite kids about learning, not drive them away from it. You play a major role in getting students enthusiastic about becoming lifelong learners. You have to bring your engagement into the classroom.

**Stop and reflect: What's your process when creating engaging lessons and experiences for your students?**

After I realized that I was the one who lacked engagement, I changed things up a bit. I completely restructured the lesson for the next few days. I took the questions from the math lesson and used them to create a game of review football, an idea I saw on Kim Bearden's Twitter page one day (@kimbearden). With the furniture pushed aside, white tape laid on the floor in one-yard increments, the kids were ready to play. I dressed in my referee uniform; my students wore the jerseys from P.E. and answered questions on their whiteboards. The game is simple: answer correctly to earn a first down and move forward. It was the same questions from the lesson, but the students' excitement skyrocketed. No more boredom or resistance to work. The best part is that the kids were learning. They worked hard, corrected mistakes, and celebrated each first down.

*Bring your engagement into the classroom!*

A big factor in the change students showed was that I was involved with them. I dressed up and dressed them up as well. I didn't sit behind the desk, barking questions at them. I was on the "field" with them. I was the ref, so I acted like it.

*Play a clean game, everyone.*

*Flag on the play! Delay of game.*

*After reviewing the play, it is determined that the students were correct. The result of the play is a touchdown!*

The results were much better. Students listened more intently. They worked with more focus. They weren't bored. They were engaged in a meaningful way because the game allowed them to do so. I was engaged with them. I was more attentive to any needs they had at the moment, which meant I could intervene on the spot if needed.

Engaging lessons with an engaging teacher will always produce good results in your students' learning.

---

The recipe for success that day: an engaging lesson and an engaged teacher. If we want better results from your students, complete a self-check first. Are we excited about our lessons? Do we show that excitement? Are our lessons engaging to the point where our kids are bummed that the lesson is over and asking for more?

*Don't settle for okay lessons when you can create great experiences.*

Asking questions of ourselves helps us find solutions in a non-condemning way. We should never be too hard on ourselves. We want to find our excitement and passion, not despair and hopelessness. Please don't be too hard on yourself. I didn't go home after that awful day and throw myself on the couch and give up. I recognized that I was to blame but refused to take the shame. I saw what the problem was and asked questions that led me to a solution. So don't beat yourself up if you're finding that you are to blame. Pick yourself up, find the solution, and execute your plan.

I've led lessons that bored me to death, and then I've taught students in ways that were exciting to everyone in the room. You can do the latter as well. You can create engaging lessons and spark excitement within your students. Don't settle for okay lessons when you can create great experiences. Your kids will be excited and grateful to you for your engagement!

**Stop and reflect: How do we balance taking responsibility for our shortcomings and getting back up and trying to be better the next day?**

# CHAPTER 4
# PASSION: A KEY INGREDIENT

There is, at least I have seen, a lot of focus on two elements of education: data-driven instruction and rigor—two important ingredients to a successful school year.

Data is a useful tool that should be guiding our instruction and interventions. Data allows us to see where our students' strengths and weaknesses lie. It helps us move forward in addressing the strengths and weaknesses of students, as well as our own. Without data, we wouldn't have the necessary information to make corrections with our students and our own teaching practices.

Rigor... Well, this one can be somewhat controversial. The *Oxford Learners Dictionary* describes rigor as "the fact of being careful and paying great attention to detail" as well as "...the difficulties and unpleasant conditions of something." These definitions of the word have the potential to spark a lively debate between teachers. One side may argue that rigor in the classroom is king; after all, being extra careful and paying attention to detail is super important. They may argue that rigor is necessary so that our kids are challenged and learn to problem solve. On the other side, there are those who believe that rigor is working our students to death, that all rigorous activities do is create frustration in our students through work that is too challenging. I'd like to think that I'm somewhere in the middle. Rigor is important for the reasons mentioned above, but too rigorous, and the kids become frustrated and check out. There's a healthy balance.

There is one ingredient that isn't talked about enough. It seems, to me, that this key ingredient gets pushed aside because the two prior ingredients are often thought of as the ones that take precedence.

That missing ingredient is passion. I'd like to take some time now to share the importance of identifying and using students' passions in our teaching, as well as our own passions.

## STUDENTS' PASSIONS.

For a long time, with such a heavy focus on data-driven instruction and rigor, Rigor RIGOR, teachers sometimes forget to recognize or even discredit the importance of our students' passions. There are kids in our schools who are passionate about video games, dancing, arts of all kinds, sports, coding, and much more. Unfortunately, they get written off. I've been guilty of that age-old saying: "Video games today are a bad influence on kids." Most people who are passionate about music, myself included, usually have a song playing in the back of their minds all day long; yet, some schools force kids to be silent in the hallways. This is hard for our students who are passionate about music, who just want to quietly sing or hum a tune. Some students are begging to make their own art, but they are told that art is not a necessary part of education, that it should be reserved for holidays. The frustration in our kids only rises when the "art" we expect them to do is basically to cut out, color, and pour glitter on a Christmas tree.

When we fail to recognize students' passions, we fail to recognize the whole individual. We begin to only see them as a warm body we have to teach, or as robots being trained to answer questions on a worksheet.

We have to start recognizing the passions of our students. Furthermore, we have to start using those passions in the classroom and giving students the opportunity to grow in their passion. In an article written by Alyssa Malmquist, she states that, "Without a passion for learning, students can lose focus and interest in completing your course—or worse, their education...Effective learning starts with learner relevance, and every subject can prove valuable once a student sees a connection between the content and their life" (*How Passionate Teaching Can Inspire Students*, 2021). Malmquist also cites a study that revealed that 45 percent of recent college dropouts left because of boredom (Johnson et al., *With Their Whole Lives Ahead of Them*, 2009). Passion is a key ingredient because it helps keep our students focused on the relevance of the content. When students can see how the content is connected to their passions, engagement is sparked, students buy into the learning, and they own it for themselves. If the topic lacks any relevance, if student passions are not brought into the lesson, this is when, for me anyway, I start to see students zone out. So let's do our best to bring their passions into the lessons we teach.

Is there a way we can use dancing as an educational tool? Sure. Use it to teach them movement, body functions, and systems. What about music? Allow students to present their knowledge of a concept in the form of a song. Can sports be used as a math tool? Absolutely. Have kids shoot a basketball from a spot repeatedly and have them graph their results as a fraction, a decimal, and a percentage. (Thanks for that wonderful lesson, Mom!) Let's start asking questions about kids' passions in order to figure out how we can use their passions to help them learn.

One year the music teacher at a school where I taught and I collaborated to help teach a young boy how to play the guitar. It was a lot of fun to watch the student develop as a musician. We often ended our lessons by sharing a song that we enjoyed. I have to give the music teacher, Mrs. Magee, a lot of credit for recognizing the musical passion buried inside this student. She also, and more importantly, deserves credit and mad props for cultivating and motivating that student to pursue his passion.

And here's another thing about this. When you include a topic or subject that the student is passionate about, the student is more likely to buy in and go all out on the assignment...rigor! I've seen the amount and quality of work students put in when they believe in the assignment they are completing. Let students rigorously explore their passions.

Recognizing students' passions also helps us to build better relationships with them. Kids care about what you're teaching them when they know you care about them. So go to their football games, their dance competitions, and ask them, with a genuine interest, about the music and games they're into. Little things like that build positive relationships with them in and out of the classroom.

**Stop and reflect: What are your students passionate about that can be used as an educational resource to teach them?**

## TEACHER PASSIONS.

It's obvious that we should include student passions in our lessons, but what about our own passions? We are part of our classrooms, so, surely, our passions have a place in all this. Teachers I talk with seem hesitant to share their passions with students for some reason. (Probably because of all that data-driven instruction and rigor.) Yet, as you are about to read, our passions definitely have a place in the classroom. We can bring our own passions to the room as a means of reaching our students.

Ever since I went shark diving in Hawaii that summer, I became passionate about sharks. I love teaching basic concepts, like identifying a character's point of view, by teaching my kids about sharks. We look at a picture of a shark and then a picture of the diver from the shark's point of view. I have the kids come up with speech bubbles for both characters to describe their points of view. We study why sharks get a bad rap. We look at why sharks are some of the fiercest creatures on the planet. I didn't *only* tell them that a great hammerhead shark can get up to 20 feet in length; we actually measured out 20 feet to put things into perspective.

One year my class looked at shark teeth that I found when visiting my brother in North Carolina. I went all out for this activity! I had our school secretary deliver a package that had no return address. She acted completely confused, and so did I. (Of course, we both knew it was something I had arranged. I knew what was inside, but I pretended to be completely confused by it.) My students wanted to know what was in it and who it was from. I decided to play dumb. I said, "Sit down, we'll open it later...although it is pretty suspicious, huh?... Hmm, oh well." The kids were dying to know immediately. So, I opened the package only to find another package inside. "Okay, now that's weird. I'll open it up after you all go to art and let you know what's inside." After a few minutes and lots of, "Mr. C., you have to open it now!" I opened up the second package. The sound of my kids when they saw another package inside of the second opened package was hilarious! I opened the third package only for my students to find something wrapped in bubble wrap. They lost it by this point! I very slowly took off the bubble wrap and revealed the container of shark teeth. I played it off to my kids and said that this was probably from my brother sending us shark teeth. "Well, kids, they look small. Should we examine them under microscopes in the science lab?" We went to the lab, and the kids analyzed them under microscopes, looking for patterns and details. The kids were buzzing by the end of the day, and they told just about every teacher and student they saw about the mysterious shark teeth.

**Stop and reflect: What are your passions? How can you incorporate them into your lessons to make them more impactful?**

What passions can you bring into the classroom to use as a teaching resource? Is there a way to bring knitting into the classroom? What about your love for football? Can you bring music into the classroom to teach poetry? If we ask enough questions and search long enough, we can all find ways to incorporate our passions into a lesson that will excite kids. It takes some thoughtful reflection, but it's possible and worth it.

Don't forget that our students are humans. So are we. When we bring our passions and theirs into the classroom, we change the narrative from robots programming robots to humans teaching humans and make school a place they love to be.

## CHAPTER 5
# WHAT THEY NEED TO HEAR

*I love you!*
*You are precious and special.*
*You are so kind to me.*
*Great job, buddy!*
*I'm proud of who you are.*

The above are some phrases that we have likely been told in our lifetime. They build us up. They encourage us. Words are pretty powerful. They paint pictures in our minds. So when we are told those things mentioned above, we see ourselves as those things.

Unfortunately, sometimes words can be really ugly.

*I hate you.*
*What's wrong with you?*
*I'm so over you.*
*How come you always mess things up?*
*You're not worth it.*

Ouch! That made me uncomfortable to even write those phrases. Again, those words paint a picture; only this time, it's not so uplifting. They tear us apart and wear us down to the bone. Those words have been used on purpose to bring others down and make them feel as if they are one of the worst human beings ever. I know because I've felt the impact of some of these words myself.

I'm sure that you, the reader, have your own list of phrases you will always remember. The truths and the lies. The helpful and hurtful. The beautiful and the ugly. Those words carry a lot of weight because of the person who spoke them to you. Perhaps a parent, a spouse, an ex, a friend, or a teacher.

Speaking of teachers, you know who really needs to be careful with what they say to students? Teachers.

I've heard stories of people who were uplifted by the words their teacher spoke to them. I've heard more stories of people who were crippled for years by what they were told by their teachers. For better or worse, we have found ourselves on the other side of a teacher's words. I hope that you are reading this remembering the good things a teacher told you, the encouragement they gave you, and how well and safe they made you feel. If you are on the opposite side of the coin, let me be the one to say that you have greatness in you, regardless of your position. You are an important piece to a complex puzzle that is your classroom and school, and without you, your kids wouldn't be the same. You are enough!

**Stop and reflect: How have you been impacted, for better or worse, by the words of your former teachers?**

We all need to be told the truth, and the truth is that we have the capability to be great. We all need to be told the things that lift our spirits and motivate us to keep up the hard work that we are doing. Our students are no exception. So many of our students believe that they are not good at math, science, or reading. They believe these things not because of past failures, but because teachers, parents, or themselves believed a little lie that was whispered (or told out loud) that their failure is part of who they are—that if they bombed a test that they aren't good at math, or that they aren't a good reader because they don't read as fast as everyone else. Then there are those students who believe that they can learn from their mistakes and improve their performance through reflection and hard work. If we want students to be excited about coming to school and to feel safe in the classroom, we need to be the ones to encourage them to keep going. We need to be the ones telling them that they are capable of greatness and that we believe in them.

There is so much more that students need to hear. Here are just a few things that students need to hear in order for their school to be a place that they love to be.

## HELLO.

Every student should be greeted. I see a lot of teachers greet their students at the door, but what about those students who pass through the halls on their way to the health office? What about the students we see running an errand to the front office? What about the students who see us as we are walking to the workroom to make copies? Those students are yours, even if they aren't in your class, and they deserve to be greeted warmly. Put yourself in the student's position. How would it make you feel to be greeted with a warm "hello" by every teacher who passed by? Probably pretty good. I can't imagine going through my day at work not being told "hello" by other teachers and my principal.

Some students come to class begging to be noticed in even the smallest ways. Some express that need in very dramatic ways. Both students want the same thing: notice me for me. The truth is, we are all longing to be noticed. A friendly greeting is one means that we use to accomplish this.

## GREET THEM BY THE NAME THEY GO BY.

A name is one of a person's first forms of identification. Before families even know the gender of their baby, they have names picked out. Names give us a sense of identity and even humanity. Why do you think the Nazis, during the Holocaust, stripped away the names of the Jewish prisoners and replaced them with a tattooed number? It robbed them of their humanity and dignity. Names are important.

Make it a point to learn the names of your students, nicknames that they want to be called, and how to correctly pronounce their names. Calling them by their names builds a better and stronger connection with your students.

One year, there were two boys who I mixed up a lot. I kept calling one by the other's name and vice versa. One of those boys was very quiet. He kept to himself most of the time in the classroom, but he did have friends he played with. He was shy in a large crowd and didn't really contribute to discussions. It kept bothering me that I couldn't make a connection with this kid. I had a thought one morning: *Maybe if you actually called him by his name, you might make a better connection.* So I decided that I would always call him by HIS name. Once I got a better handle on this, the student began to open up, participate more, and even talk with me during lunch or recess. Just by calling him by his name, this student showed drastic improvement in his participation and interaction.

> *Calling them by their names builds a better and stronger connection with your students.*

As mentioned earlier, all the students are our students. You may not be able to remember every student's name, but at least try. Calling them by their name gives you an opportunity to connect with them, and it makes them feel respected. We demand that students call us by our correct names. We should treat them with the same respect that we expect from them.

One year a student walked into my classroom on Meet Your Teacher Day. When the mom introduced herself, I recognized her last name as one of the students on my list. Here's how my first interaction with this student went.

*Me: Hi! You must be Emiliya (pronounced Eh-mee-lee-uh).*

*Student (as polite and sweet as she could be): No. Emiliya (pronounced Em-i-lee-yuh).*

Students do care how you say their name. It's so important to let them correct us when we botch saying their name or misspell it. And giving kids nicknames because we can't say their name is not okay. If they didn't ask you for that nickname, avoid doing this. Instead...learn their name!

If you have students with cultural names that may be difficult to pronounce, I suggest spending a few moments each day just practicing saying the name and spelling it. One year I had a student with a name I had never heard of. It wasn't spelled at all the way I thought it would be when I heard it. To learn how to pronounce it, I asked the student for the correct pronunciation, and then I would practice at random times (walking to the copier, in between bites at lunch, etc.). Nothing formal, but I still practiced. I also asked the student if I pronounced their name correctly when I spoke with them. After a while, I had no trouble pronouncing the student's name. As for spelling, I had to treat it like a sight word. I'm not trying to say that I reduced their name to a sight word like "said," but I used the same strategy I teach my kids to use when it comes to words that don't follow any phonetic rules...memorization. The only way, for me, was to memorize how to spell it, just like a student learns to spell a sight word. If you have students with cultural names that may be difficult to pronounce, it's extremely important to learn how to say their full names with the correct pronunciation. You honor them and their families by doing this.

Speaking of families, it's a great idea to ask families about the name of their child. Whether it's a name you are unfamiliar with or perhaps a name not spelled phonetically correct, a parent took time to think about and decide on their child's name. One way we can honor our students and families is by asking about the story and significance behind our students' names.

## TELL ME HOW YOU ARE FEELING/DOING TODAY.

Along with greeting every student by name, follow-up phrases such as "how are you feeling today" go a long way to building a positive relation-ship with our students. It shows students that you care about their well-being. You aren't just greeting them out of formality, but you are greeting them because you are genuinely concerned about how they are doing.

It's very simple, yet it's very powerful. It opens up doors for conversations. I've had students break down and cry when I asked them how they were doing, explaining a heartache that no one (especially a fourth-grade student) should have to experience. I have had students tell me how great they are feeling and how happy they are because they got good news earlier that day. You just never know. Please ask how they are doing.

## I'M PROUD OF WHO YOU ARE.

Some kids are waiting for someone to tell them that who they are as an individual is special. They are waiting for someone to see them as more than just a student in the classroom; they are waiting for someone to see them as the individual they are. They want to know that you are proud of who they are. "I'm proud of you" is a simple phrase, but it carries a tremendous impact. It builds them up and gives them confidence. I know that because it works for you and me. Even when my students mess up, I can still be proud of them. I'm not necessarily proud of what they might have done, but it doesn't change who they are. I can always be proud of who they are as an individual.

## I'M SORRY.

I once wrongly accused a student while yelling at him for something that I thought he had done. To be honest, I don't even remember what I was upset about—proof that it wasn't even something worth getting upset over. I was irate, though. When I realized that it wasn't the student's fault, that it was a freak glitch with technology, I felt so humiliated. I knew I had to apologize. I sat down and apologized to the student directly in front of the entire class. It was embarrassing, and I could feel my face getting warm as I said the words, "I'm sorry. I was way out of line. Please forgive me." Those words went a long way, though. That student was one of the hardest-working students I taught that year. I attribute that to the apology I made to him and the trust it built. Sincere apologies help heal the relationship. If you keep your word moving forward, then trust is built.

*We need to be quick to apologize when we are at fault.*

Some teachers don't like to admit when we are wrong. It's always the students' or parents' or the administrators' fault, right? The students' scores? The students' behavior? Not everything that happens with our students is our fault, but it's not always their fault either. Even if it is, let's not forget that they are humans, just like us, making mistakes from time to time. We need to be quick to apologize when we are at fault and have grace for them when they are at fault.

**Stop and reflect: Of the phrases mentioned above, which do you tell students most often? Which positive phrase will you try to say more often?**

---

There's so much more that kids deserve to hear on a daily basis. I'm sure you can think of some things that students need to hear that I didn't mention. If you have other ideas of things that students need to hear, please share what you think kids need to hear on your social media platforms using the hashtag #APlaceTheyLoveBook. Not on social media? Perhaps you can have a discussion with a colleague and reflect together. Telling kids the things that they need and deserve to hear goes a long way toward making school a place that they love to be at.

**Stop and reflect: Write three (or more if you'd like) phrases that
kids need to hear.**

1:

2:

3:

# CHAPTER 6
# SORRY, FUN FRIDAY'S OVER

I got a letter from a former student once. Student letters always make me excited, whether from former or current students—only this letter was more than an "I miss you" letter.

In the letter, the student stated that she missed being in my class and that she hoped I was having a good year so far. She mentioned that my students are very lucky to have me. This is where the letter took a different turn. She continued by saying that she hoped that my kids realized that I was a teacher who believed in having fun and that I am a good teacher because I don't make my kids do boring things.

It saddened me to read this, knowing that there are students like her who are practically begging to learn in a fun and exciting way. There are students in our classrooms, schools, and districts who are bored to death because they had to do another worksheet. Then there are the students, like the one I am about to mention, who are eager for "Fun Friday" to arrive.

A student of mine asked me, during his first week with me, if we would have Fun Fridays. I had never heard of Fun Friday... I had questions for this kid. He said that at his last school, they would work hard all week and have nothing but fun activities on Friday.

Why is that a thing? Why is the fun reserved for Fridays? Why don't schools have fun on a daily basis?

Somewhere in the past, I believe, educators bought into the lie that if it's fun, then it's not educational. They believed that good education looks like worksheet packets that are "rigorous," and a silent class is a class that is learning. Somewhere we fell into a trap that teaches us that fun is reserved for one day out of the week or for the holidays. My question is this: why can't meaningful learning and fun be coupled together? I believe that they can and that they should.

One reason I think teachers settle (yes, settle) for the boring activity or lesson is that it's easy. It's easy to print worksheets and hand those to kids. One of my former principals used to call them "shut up sheets" because behind every worksheet is the hope that our students will shut up, finish the worksheet, and ask for another one. (They won't, by the way, ask for another one.)

Unfortunately, this creates laziness and a lack of problem-solving skills among our students. I had a handful of "worksheet kids" once. When tasked with something like completing a puzzle or creating a game on Code.org, the students were completely lost. They needed another student or me to walk them through almost every step.

I'm not that teacher who will hold students' hands through something like that, so I would ask them questions like: "What haven't you tried?" "What action have you used that is causing your game to not code correctly?"

None of them could answer me with anything but "I don't know. Can you just help me, please?"

During a math lesson using gamification, three students told me that they would rather have a worksheet because it wasn't as hard. That's the result of a teacher who has handed them worksheets every day, all year long.

They also struggled with self-regulation and self-pacing. My assistant principal had observed me teaching poetry, point of view, and theme through song lyrics, as I mentioned in the chapter "Ready. Set. Bring It!". I was dressed up as John Lennon, singing Beatles music and discussing the lyrics with my kids. Ultimately, the students needed to select a song of their own to analyze and present. Her feedback was that my lesson and delivery were awesome, but she was still frustrated. She couldn't understand why my kids didn't have more self-control or why they couldn't participate in a group discussion or stay focused on the long-term goal. These kids she was referring to were the "worksheet kids."

I had noticed this for a long time myself, but it was pretty eye-opening to my assistant principal. When I explained what some of them had told me about preferring a worksheet over a highly engaging and interactive lesson, she couldn't believe her ears. All of a sudden it made sense to her: "worksheet kids" aren't being trained to participate in group work or discussions, especially when self-pacing is required, and they have trouble knowing how to self-regulate.

Another reason teachers don't strive for more fun and engaging lessons is due to the misunderstanding that fun is the dog-and-pony show. I don't blame them for that one. No one can possibly bring out the bells and whistles every day for six hours a day, maintain a life outside of school, take care of themselves, and stay sane. Those lessons can take a lot of time and energy to create and prepare. So instead of searching for little things to do that make the learning more fun, we settle for mediocre worksheets and a boring popcorn read-aloud.

Teachers, it's time to ditch the worksheet and the boring. We are not doing our students any favors by having them sit quietly and fill in the blanks. They aren't truly having fun, and they aren't learning valuable prosocial behaviors. We definitely aren't making school a place that they love.

## SO WHAT DO WE DO ABOUT WORKSHEETS?

One thing I can't stand is worksheets. Worksheets are often used as a form of "assessment," an "activity," or anything else that sounds important or fun. Now, I admit, I still use them. I find that they can serve as decent practice for students working toward mastery, as long as the questions and tasks are aligned to curricular standards. I know, though, worksheets aren't fun...unless you cut up the questions and hide them around the room for students to find. It's not uncommon to step into my room to find students looking under the desks or chairs, looking behind the window blinds, inside dictionaries, behind anchor charts, and in other nooks and crannies trying to find hidden questions from a boring old worksheet. This scavenger hunt idea also works with task cards, too. Yes, students can leave them in a pile and answer them one by one in numerical order. But will they go home and talk about that? I doubt it. Will they go home and talk about how they answered a question that was taped underneath a table or hidden behind the pencil sharpener? Yes!

## BABY STEPS

How do we make school a fun place to be at? Baby steps. It's the little things that we can do that make learning fun—such as pictures and music.

As useful and important as grammar is, I despise teaching it. I find it so boring, and for years, my students did too. I was stuck and didn't know how to make it fun. Then one year I got an idea from CJ Reynolds when I heard him speak at the 2019 Teach Better Conference about using relevant images and music for vocabulary words. I figured that I could easily apply the same idea to something as boring as teaching nouns. I started using images from Fortnite, Minecraft, The Avengers, and more to help kids identify nouns. The lesson right after possessive nouns was all about common and proper nouns. I decided to use an image of one of the most popular villains ever: Darth Vader. The image was perfect. The lights were turned off, and there stood Vader, steam rising from under his feet, a red glow from his lightsaber illuminating his shadowy figure. My kids had the task of writing a sentence for the image, underlining the proper possessive noun, and circling the common noun. Simple, I know, but I was about to add a little excitement. Kids were really getting to it. After they wrote their sentences, they were ready to share aloud what they wrote. "Hold on," I said. This is where it got fun. I queued up some dramatic music: The Imperial March. Oh, it was on! They read their sentences about Darth Vader's lightsaber with his theme song playing, and it was epic! Every kid wanted to participate now. It wasn't anything that was hard or over the top, but it took something boring like grammar and made it fun.

**Stop and reflect: What is one baby step that you can take today to make tomorrow's lesson fun?**

## TAKE THEM OUTSIDE.

There is so much that teachers do within their own four walls, but we still have our limits. That's why a lot of educators, just like you, take their students outside to learn. Changing the environment is a great way to mix things up, but more importantly, it opens opportunities for students to experience something happening in the moment. Plus, it's a lot of fun!

I love it when it rains or snows. I love the smell of rain and the sound of snow crunching beneath my feet. In New Mexico, we don't get much rain and snow throughout the year, so those forms of precipitation are cherished. During the school year, I always take my students outside after a rain or snow storm. One activity I do is to have students write the questions, "Where does water go, and what does it take with it?" in their notebooks. Then we move outside to different locations (the playground, the bus lane, walkways, etc.) and write or draw what we see. When we do this, students usually begin to form their own questions, one of the most common being, "Where did all this trash come from?"

Another time I asked students who could make a snowball melt the fastest. We went outside so the students could do something simple: melt a snowball. But it was more than that. They could only use things in their environment, nothing from inside. This taught concepts like winter survival skills, but it was also a chance for students to practice thinking critically.

I've let my students write poetry with chalk outside as a display for other students to admire. I've done a similar activity with chalk where students showed off their knowledge of fractions, displaying number lines, equivalent fractions, and more diagrams of fractions. I've taken my students outside for activities such as observing clouds and identifying areas where root wedging has taken place. There is a lot you can do outside, so if you are looking to spice things up with some fun and excitement, try taking them outside for a rocking experience.

## FUN BRAIN BREAKS.

We all deserve a break from work. Even if it's just a minute long, brain breaks have been found to improve focus, promote positive behavior, and even improve higher-level thinking. An article posted on *Edutopia* (Terada, "Research-Tested Benefits of Breaks," 2018) claims that:

Regular breaks throughout the school day—from short brain breaks in the classroom to the longer break of recess—are not simply downtime for students. Such breaks increase their productivity and provide them with opportunities to develop creativity and social skills...Breaks keep our brains healthy and play a key role in cognitive abilities such as reading comprehension and divergent thinking (the ability to generate and make sense of novel ideas).

So we know that brain breaks are important, but they are also a lot of fun. Here's a list of brain break ideas that you can utilize in the classroom today.

- Take a nap for ___ seconds
- Draw/doodle for ___ seconds/minutes
- Exercise (jog in place, pushups, jumping jacks, etc.)
- Snowball Fight (students crumble up a piece of paper into a ball and have a "snowball fight" in the classroom)
- Bullseye (similar to Snowball Fight, students throw their "snowball" at a target that you can draw on your chalkboard or whiteboard)
- Plug your nose singing (sing a song while holding your nose closed)
- Do the Wave
- Drum solo (students perform their best "drum" solo by tapping pencils on the desks for ___ seconds)
- Lightsabers (students have a pretend lightsaber battle with their invisible lightsabers)
- Zombie Tag (students *walk* like a zombie to tag another zombie)
- Tiptoe Tag (students *walk* on their tiptoes to tag another player)

- Rock Band (get the music cranking and let your students play air guitar, bass guitar, and other instruments in the song you play)
- Freeze Dance (students dance while you play a song but freeze when you pause the music)
- Share a joke with another classmate and listen to their joke
- Play short games like Hangman or Simon Says

If you have other ideas for brain breaks, please share them with your colleagues and on social media.

## CHANGE UP THE LEARNING STYLE.

Can students learn from you every day if all you do is lecture? Maybe, but that gets old, and you may not hold their attention very long. How many times have you heard a student say, "Ah, we have to do this again?" I understand that re-reading is important. I do a lot of re-reads. But I will change up how it's done in order to keep students engaged. For example, I might read the text with students in small groups, but complete the re-read the next day as a whole class so the text can be discussed as a whole class. I have even done a re-re-read, where students read the text with a partner and complete an appropriate activity.

Sometimes those activities are answering questions. Sometimes it will require students to ask the questions. Other times, it's completing the work using one of the many Google Apps or Seesaw, Nearpod, or Kahoot. Instead of showing students a number line, I hand my students numbers on a card, a long and thick piece of string, and clothespins; from there, they can experience creating their own number line instead of plotting the numbers on the number line in a workbook. Not that there's anything inherently wrong about plotting numbers on a number line in a workbook; mix it up, is what I'm saying. (More on this in the chapter "Keep it Fresh.")

**Stop and reflect: Fun isn't all bells and whistles, but it can be. Have you created a lesson that some might say is "over the top?" What did you do?**

---

Teachers, we need to find as many ways to make our schools a fun place to be. Yes, students' primary goal is to learn, but why can't they learn while having fun? It makes our jobs fun too. As I said, I hate teaching grammar. The day I started using images and music during my lesson, though, I actually got excited to teach that lesson! Remember, our schools should be places that everyone—students and teachers—love to be.

Our kids might be learning, but are they having fun? We can't sell them tickets to the opera when they want to go see a punk rock show. They want the energy and excitement of a Green Day concert, not Madame Butterfly. We need to bring it to them. They will be grateful to us when we put an end to Fun Friday and make every day a day to have fun.

---

*From Scarlett Jones (13) - Former Student of Elijah Carbajal*

Having fun at school is important because school shouldn't be a place that people dread to go to every day. We should want to go to school every day to learn and enjoy ourselves. School was never meant to be a jail for kids six hours a day, Monday through Friday. It was supposed to be a fun place for kids to go, but our world has turned into a place where far too often, you hear kids saying things like, "School was horrible today. All we did was sit at our desks quietly and take a boring old test. I hate school! I'm never going again! School is the worst place in the world!" Aren't you ever tired of hearing kids say things like that?

Instead, we should be hearing things like, "School was great today! We got to learn point of view by our teacher dressing up as famous people and teaching us what those people think about a certain subject. I love school! School is the best place in the world!"

I have heard kids say that "school" stands for Six Cruel Hours Of

Our Lives. I have also heard kids say that "test" stands for Testing/Taking Every Student's Time. Instead, I should hear Six Cool Hours Of Our Lives. Our future rests in the hands of the kids that have to go to school. If they hate it, our future will be a very bad one because none of them would have paid attention in school, and then they would all be stupid. Because really, school should be a fun and exciting place, not a dreadful and horrible place.

A time that I learned something important while having fun is when I was in 4th grade. I was 9. My teacher was Mr. Carbajal. One day, we were all lining up outside to go in when our teacher, Mr. Carbajal, got in front of us in a wig and funky glasses. We asked him why he was wearing what he was, and he said you'll see. So, when we got into class, he said, "I am John Lennon from the Beatles. Your teacher, Mr. Carbajal, told me to walk you in here and teach you about an author's point of view." We all knew that it was our teacher, but he said that he was John Lennon, so there we were, learning point of view while the whole time our teacher was claiming that he was John Lennon. This happened multiple times that year. He dressed up like rock star, Jon Cooper, and like country music star, Eric Church.

Another time that I learned something important while having fun was when we had taped white tape in horizontal strips all across the floor. My teacher had a referee shirt, and we borrowed green and yellow jerseys from our P.E. teacher, Ms. Eighme. Our teacher would assign us teams, and we would either sit or stand at the beginning line on our defensive side with our curriculum books and whiteboards. Our teacher would project questions onto the screen, and we would look in our books if we needed them, and write down our answers on our whiteboards. Once our teacher said, we would show our whiteboards, and whoever got it right would move to the next line, and whoever got it wrong would stay. We would have to wait for all our team members to come to the same line we were on before we moved forward. Once we got to the offensive side, we had a "touchdown," and we would do a victory dance. We would move our desks and get the yellow and green jerseys very often to play this. We called this football.

My experience of learning about a character's point of view the way I was taught and of playing "football" made school more fun and enjoyable for me because I saw that school could be more than just sitting at a desk and taking a test. I saw that school could be fun and enjoyable. I saw that school could become a place that *I would want to wake up at 6:00 in the morning* to go to, six hours a day, Monday through Friday. It became a place that I would want to go to and be at.

When I was in fifth grade, I also had an experience that not only told me that school was one of my favorite places to be but also showed me how much I love school. I was 10, and my teachers were Ms. Thornhill and Mr. Ober. School was closed for the rest of the year in April due to the worldwide disaster that was called Coronavirus, or Covid-19. We had to do Zoom meetings on the computer and do our work from Google Classroom at home. We were in quarantine. When I heard that school was closed for the rest of the year, I cried. I just could not forget all the great memories that made fifth grade the best school year of my life. I remember every time that I turned on the T.V., I would see Covid-19: more news, Covid-19: how to try to stop the spread, Covid-19: what you need to know, Covid-19: we need more hospital beds and bigger hospitals. I also remember one night, my family and I were eating at the dinner table when we started talking about the Coronavirus. They said that when you get older, you will look back on this time in your life and be able to tell people that you lived through the Coronavirus. I asked why that was so important, and they said because the Coronavirus will be one of the worst things in worldwide history. All this just showed me even more how much I love school.

The advice that I have for teachers when it comes to making

learning fun is you need to know what kids enjoy. When I was in 4th grade, Mr. Carbajal created a cafe in our classroom. It was called Café Carbel. Whenever we walked into class Friday morning, there would be black tablecloths and flowerpots with flowers on the tables. There would usually be parents in there that brought snacks. We would get to just sit and talk at our tables while we worked, and Mr. Carbajal and other parent volunteers would come over to us and ask us what drink we wanted! Could you do something like that, or would you just give them a paper to work on?

Also, you need to remember that happiness is the key to success. So, if you want successful students, you should think up something (it doesn't even have to be that big or grand) that would make your students smile in class. Remember, a big heart leads to a big smile that leads to big success. (Did I just make up a new saying?!) Teachers, if you make school fun, then there will be a whole lot more people who enjoy school in the world.

# CHAPTER 7
# CELEBRATING KIDS OUTSIDE OF SCHOOL

I f you have a family, a second job, or any other responsibilities after your day job as an intelligent and creative educator, you may have wanted to skip over this chapter. I understand. Doing this when you have a family, especially your own children, may be downright impossible. Hang on, though. I have some tips for how you can still celebrate your students for their out-of-school activities.

I'd venture to say that every teacher knows just how important it is to celebrate student success. Rejoicing with them when they pass a test with flying colors or calling home to tell families just how well their student is doing goes a long way to developing positive relationships with our students and families. It boosts students' confidence in the classroom and motivates them to continue working hard.

I was homeschooled. My mom, a former special education teacher, taught me, my four brothers, and my little sister from kindergarten through twelfth grade. (My mom is one of my education heroes. Love you, Mom!) I'll never forget the day I passed a math test with 100%. My mom grabbed me by the hand and started celebrating with me! It makes me happy to think about how excited my mom was for me. She celebrated my hard work with me at that moment, and it makes me want to do the same for my students. They deserve to know that I am proud of them for their efforts.

Students also deserve to be celebrated outside of the classroom. They spend a huge chunk of the year in our classrooms, but they still have lives outside the four walls of our rooms. They are not students first and then everything else. Being a student is part of who they are, but they are also athletes, dancers, farmers, gamers, hunters, musicians, and much more. As educators, we need to see that as a crucial part of who they are and celebrate that.

**Stop and reflect: When were you, as a student, celebrated outside of school? What impact did it have on you?**

## WHAT IF I CAN'T MAKE IT TO THE EVENT?

*Elijah, I have a husband, two little children, and three dogs. What you are suggesting and recommending is almost impossible. I can't put my family aside like that.*

You're right. Your family is always number one, or at least they should be. I would never encourage anyone to put their job or even their students over their own family. It's still important to celebrate the students outside of school. I have some suggestions.

My first suggestion is to start with a phone call or text message to the family. One year, my weekends were being used for personal matters, which meant I couldn't attend many sporting events. My students asked me repeatedly to go, to which I explained that I couldn't. It didn't stop me from calling their family to ask how the game went. By calling or texting, the family understood that I was interested in their child's interests and passions. Even though I couldn't be there, I could call and wish the student good luck before their game. So can you. Contacting the families via phone calls, text messages, emails, or many of the other communication apps that teachers and families use lets families know something important: You care about their child.

The second thing I recommend if you are unable to go to an out-of-school event for a student is to celebrate that student inside the classroom for what they accomplish outside the classroom. When your student comes in to let you know she won her volleyball game, celebrate with her and the class with a quick victory dance! Let the students know that you take pride in what they do outside of the classroom.

I'd also recommend that you bring what they do outside the classroom into the classroom. I had students who really enjoyed learning about outer space. I transformed a mini-unit about the phases of the moon by dressing like an astronaut, giving the students a hands-on activity to teach the phases of the moon and what causes the phases, and even bringing in another teacher with extensive knowledge of the NASA Space Camp program. Other times, I turned my review days into game days, like football, skeeball, and other stuff I saw the kids doing during recess. Basically, if the kids are into it, and if it's appropriate for the classroom, bring it in. It demonstrates that you notice your students, even if you can't always go to their out-of-school events.

**Stop and reflect: Is there a way to harness and celebrate what kids are involved in outside of the classroom inside your classroom to build positive relationships?**

## A TALE OF TWO STUDENTS.

Let me tell you about a couple of students. The first is a young girl I taught in my fifth year of teaching. This young girl and her family are Christians who uphold the Jewish feasts and traditions, while still recognizing Jesus as the Son of God. This young girl invited another teacher and me to her family's church celebration of Hanukkah. When I showed up, you should have seen this girl's face. My students always create secret handshakes to use when we greet each other. Not that night. She ran up to greet me with a smile and a hug! I sat with her, her family, and the other teacher who went with me, listened closely as her mom explained the traditions taking place. I witnessed, before my own eyes, this girl laugh as she took all my chocolate in a game of Dreidel.

That girl was so excited that we were there to take part in traditions that make her who she is. Her family has continued to invite me to all of their events and traditions, which I've been lucky enough to attend even after this student moved on to the next grade level. Why would she continue to invite me, and why would I do all that, even throughout the summer and after she moves to a new grade level with a new teacher? Because she knows that I truly care about her. Because I enjoy celebrating kids outside of school. I care about who she is as a person, not just as a student.

Secondly, I taught a young boy who was an athlete through and through. He wrestled, played football, and played baseball. He was also a squirrely little fellow; he liked to talk over people, liked to be the center of attention, and occasionally would get very little work done due to too much socializing with other kids. I had some difficulty motivating him, especially during my writing block—until I went to one of his football games. I noticed a huge change in behavior after spending an afternoon cheering him on during a Saturday football game. I noticed the behavior got even better when I went to two of his baseball games and his wrestling match. I also started playing games with him at school, like tetherball or kickball. He was getting more work done, and it was much better quality work. I credit that to me going to his games, spending more time with him outside of my classroom, and with the intentional relationship-building steps I took.

———

A lot of times, all it takes is going to one event outside of school to start making a difference in the lives of kids. Those deep relationships we want with students might begin to develop because you decided to attend a football game. Relationships matter. Deeper relationships lead to happier and more confident students. Better relationships with students mean so much. Students will work harder for you because they know you care. Student behaviors will be better, meaning students will work harder, follow you instead of just following rules, and they will be calmer and happier.

I believe that we can make school a place they love to be when we celebrate them in the other places of their lives—churches, sports complexes, dance studios, and more—places where they love to be. Because when you celebrate the person, not just the student that they are, trust is built. The relationships become stronger and more genuine. So what are you waiting for? Go to that football game. Go to the ballet recital. Go watch for them in the city parade. Ask frequently about their out-of-school activities and bring what they are passionate about into the classroom. You'll be amazed at how much they appreciate you for it.

## CHAPTER 8
# KEEP IT FRESH

I was hanging out with a couple of teacher friends, along with the son of one of those teachers one night in the mall. (We aren't big-time mall shoppers, so we were actually there for the son.) We walked into a store that the boy wanted to check out. As we walked in, we were greeted by an employee of the store. That employee immediately started talking to the boy, saying that he looked "fresh" in his new Champion clothing.

Fresh. It's a word used to describe something new and stylish, such as clothing or a haircut, but it can (at least, I think) be applied to almost anything new. In today's culture, that's what we are going for: fresh! Out with the old and in with the new. You can probably tell where this is about to go.

While there are lessons that I like to teach every year, I've never been that teacher that laminates lesson plans and sticks them in a filing cabinet. I'm not a hoarder as it is, and I'm much more likely to save a file on Google Drive anyway. Whether it's laminated or an electronic file, I'm still not one to use the same lessons year after year after year. Even when I do, the delivery is usually different based on my current students' needs.

Do you get tired of teaching the same thing year after year? Keep it fresh. Stop using the same materials and lessons you used in year one during your 20th year of teaching. I can honestly say that I teach differently now than I did my first, second, or even my third year, and with each new year that follows something new is added to my teaching style or the way I deliver content. I want to stay fresh.

## KIDS ARE CHANGING. WHY AREN'T WE?

Some teachers are using the same lessons they taught years ago. Those laminated lesson plans are regurgitated along with the expectation that they will go the same as they did 10 years ago. News flash: it might not go as well as you think it will.

Our students are changing. The music they listen to is much different from the music I grew up listening to. They can listen to my music, like Green Day, The Beatles, Skillet, or August Burns Red, but it's not particularly what they are into. They like Justin Bieber, Ariana Grande, and other pop artists. I listen to bands; they listen to artists. I like punk rock, classic rock, and metal; they like pop music, Lo-Fi, and EDM. I like rap music. They like "rap" music. (The real OGs know what I mean!) They haven't seen the movies we watched. One day I showed my students a picture of Heath Ledger's Joker from The Dark Knight...they had no idea which Batman film that was from. They recognized the Joker's makeup and outfit but didn't realize who was behind the makeup. My mind was blown—I must be getting old.

The way they learn is different. They were born after smartphones, the Internet, WiFi, and Netflix became a thing. They don't know what Block-buster and answering machines are — I mean, were. They learn by asking Siri or Google a question. They also learn by just trying things, i.e., exploring. They skip the video game tutorials and try things, learning the controls and tricks as they go along. They don't learn from an hour-long lecture followed up by worksheet packets. The way our students learn is different from the way we taught them five years ago. So why are we teaching the same way with the same lessons and expecting the same result? Why are we expecting our kids to take risks and try learning new things if we aren't willing to do the same? It's extremely hypocritical. Tell me if these phrases sound familiar:

*I just don't get that whole social media thing. I can't figure it out.*
*It's the way we all learned it, so why can't they?*
*I want to use _____, but I'm not tech-savvy.*
*I don't have time to figure out how to _____.*
*I have used this for the last few years. Why isn't it working? Why aren't they getting it?*

Whether you and I are guilty of saying them to others or not (which I am), the fact is that those are excuses for not trying new things. We constantly want our kids to be brave, take risks, and try something new, even if they fail. My question to you is this: when was the last time you were brave, took a risk, and tried something new, even if you failed?

**Stop and reflect: When was the last time you tried something fresh in your classroom? What did you learn from that experience?**

## SOMETHING BESIDES A WORKSHEET.

Our kids get excited when we try new things. A student once told me, "You're the best teacher ever because you are creative, and you try things that other teachers aren't doing." One of the best compliments ever; however, I have to admit that I have sometimes done what's easier. I've fallen back on what is familiar and easy. It's easier to use the old than to explore ideas for something new, and I have fallen into that trap.

Again, we can't expect that what worked one year will work the next. Maybe it will to some extent, but I would bet that it needs some refining to meet your new students' needs. It should be our goal to speak the language of our kids. They need teachers who keep things fresh.

So what can we use instead of a worksheet? Platforms like Seesaw (web.seesaw.me/) offer different options for students to use when submitting work, such as creating audio or video recordings, typing their responses, or drawing or adding a picture to their answers. There's more than just Seesaw. Another good platform to use is Nearpod. Nearpod is chock full of lessons, but you also have the ability to create your own lessons using the Nearpod features. Some of those features include games like matching cards (similar to the old card game Memory), open-ended questions, and drawing or attaching photos as an answer. I would also recommend reading *Create* by Bethany Petty (2020). She offers lots of resources, including free templates, that give students a chance to express their voice through student choice.

## BRING IN AN EXPERT.

You could also bring in experts. In *The Expert Effect* (Grayson McKinney and Zach Rondot, 2021), teachers find encouragement from the authors to bring experts into the classroom. I remember one year, my students were learning about weather patterns. Some of the activities were great, but I wanted to do something that would get the kids excited. McKinney and Grayson say, "The wonderful thing about finding experts...is that it takes some of the pressure off of you! You don't have to pretend to be an expert at something you're not" (p. 35). So, I took an idea from that chapter (p. 34) because it fit perfectly with what my students were learning; I reached out to a local meteorologist, Steve Stucker, and I asked if he would give a presentation to our third-grade class even if it wasn't their current unit of study. He said yes, and he came to our school one morning to deliver his presentation. His presentation had the students really engaged and enthusiastic that day! The students appreciated not only seeing someone who is on T.V. but learning from a professional who was able to show how education, especially science, is used in a real way. Bringing in experts is a great way to keep things fresh.

One year I coordinated with Dennis Mathew (@storiesbydennis), the author of *Bello the Cello*, *My Wild First Day of School*, and *How Grizzly Found Gratitude*, to visit our school, read one of his books (he went with *Bello the Cello*—a fantastic book!), sing music inspired by the stories, and talk about what it's like to be an author. Normally, Dennis does his presentation live, but this took place during the COVID-19 pandemic, so the presentation was virtual. Still, Dennis was super animated, engaging, and exciting. He did all the things I mentioned, and he was even able to connect us (virtually) with another musician who played the cello for the students! To top it off, our school had enough funding to purchase a copy of *Bello the Cello* for every student. It was an incredible experience! Whether your expert is live or virtual, they make a huge difference when they are with your students.

## EXPERTS AMONG US.

As your students learn the objectives we so eagerly teach, it might be a good idea to mix up your assessment piece. Throw the stale, expired work page away. Let them show off their knowledge and expertise in various ways. I mentioned Seesaw as a way of recording answers instead of selecting a multiple-choice option. This option allows students to be the expert with a familiar audience: their classmates and their family. This is always a great place to start because the audience is someone your students will be comfortable with.

When you and your students are ready for a larger audience, might I suggest a podcast or blog post. One year, I mentioned to my students that I host a podcast called "The Shut Up and Teach Podcast." They were interested, and a few asked if they could be guests on the show. I asked if they would rather be on my show or have their classroom podcast. The excitement rose tremendously! The class was buzzing. I created a podcast using Anchor.fm, sent permission slips home, and in a short time, "The Everything Podcast" was created. Students generated ideas for the podcast that included discussions about football, the water cycle, multiplication chants, math concepts, gardening, gaming, and more. My students put so much effort and focus into this podcast because of the audience they were potentially reaching and because it was something they could actually get excited about. *(The podcast is now called "The Student Expert Podcast." You can listen to their episodes on most major platforms. We hope you will listen!)*

## STUDENT INTERESTS.

What about using what they are into as a means of reaching them? On a few occasions, I have played the music videos from some of their favorite songs to teach about nouns and verbs. They would watch the video first, watch it again while reading the lyric sheet, and lastly identify some of the nouns and verbs mentioned or seen. I said earlier that I hate teaching grammar, but those days were fun. The kids enjoyed it, too, because it was something that they could connect with. It made the content relevant. It was fresh! It was simple, but it made all the difference.

When I started podcasting with my students, they really began to show their interests. Being allowed to share their passions and interests with a larger audience was very useful when it came to discovering student interests. Giving the students choice in what they wanted to talk about on the podcast opened up the door for them to really dive in.

## GOING TECH-LESS.

*Tests don't have to be given on paper or as a Google Form.*

Assessments and lessons don't have to include technology. Have you ever given a student scissors and a magazine? Once I asked students to cut and paste (not on a computer) pictures from a magazine that demonstrated different forms of energy and to organize them by pasting them onto a large piece of construction paper. I didn't ask them to answer questions on a Google Form. I gave them a chance to think critically, apply their understanding in a deeper way, and...did I mention that students got to cut and glue pictures from magazines onto construction paper? Based on their reaction, my students didn't get to do that very much in the past. They were so engaged that they were shocked when I told them that this was their assessment.

Other times, I've done snowball activities. This one is kind of old school, but it's still effective. I have the students create a question about the text or content that we are learning. They write their question on a piece of paper without writing their name unless they choose to. Then they crumble up their papers, and they have a "snowball fight," tossing crumpled paper balls at each other. At the end, everyone has a question that is most likely not their own. This strategy is, first of all, fun! Kids love the movement break. Second, this takes pressure off of students who may be too shy to ask a question they actually have. Now someone else is asking their question, and they get to ask someone else's question. No pressure, right? Third, it opens up the door for great discussions, which gives you a chance to teach social skills like taking turns, using an appropriate speaking voice, etc. It works as an informal assessment, like a check-in, while your students are discussing and sharing their knowledge of the content.

Art is a terrific option for students to demonstrate their knowledge, especially for subjects like language arts and social studies. Sometimes my students will ask to paint/draw a picture that recreates what they read or learned about during the lesson. I even had a student complete a piece of art during math, in order to explain the concept of fractions. I try to include games in my lessons as much as I can. Games including cards, dice, base-ten blocks, toy money, or other manipulatives can greatly enhance the learning of your students.

Tests don't have to be given on paper or as a Google Form. If we continue to push ourselves and think creatively, we can continue to keep things fresh for our learners, with or without technology.

**Stop and reflect: If you realized your teaching strategies, activities, and practices are past the expiration date, what change would you make to keep it fresh?**

We have to keep in mind that we are not there for ourselves. Yes, it's our job, it's how we make a living, but that's not *why* we do what we do. Schools are built for students, not for adults. We are here to make school a place that they love to be so that they can learn and become equipped for life. We need to reach and teach our students, but we don't do that by using outdated teaching methods and 10-year-old lesson plans. We have to keep it—our delivery, mentality, and outreach—fresh!

It's not that we need to reinvent the wheel, but wheels, at some point, need to be serviced. Do your educational wheels need to be serviced? How so? Maybe all it will take is getting connected with other educators on Twitter or other social media platforms. Connect with me on Twitter and Instagram. Just search for @carbaeli, #ShutUpAnd Teach, and/or #APlace-TheyLoveBook. I would love to connect with you and share ideas. You can also participate in Twitter chats. Even searching for hashtags such as #TeachBetter, #tlap, or #CrazyPLN can connect you with incredible educators. You will find other educators just like you to connect with and help you keep things fresh in your classroom. Get connected with other teachers in your school, even if they aren't teaching your grade level or content. (Sometimes, you learn more from those outside of your content area than those inside of it.)

Do all that you can do to make and keep things fresh. You'll find joy in teaching again. Your kids will find joy in learning. Both of you will discover that school is a place that you love.

**Stop and reflect: Who can you connect with, either at your school or on social media, to help give you fresh ideas?**

# CHAPTER 9
# *SHUT UP AND TEACH*

Before I say anything else, I want to say that I am in no way belittling any problems or issues you may be facing. What you are dealing with is real, and you have the right to feel every emotion that comes with that. Some of our issues are huge: depression, anxiety, vehicle trouble, broken relationships, financial crisis, infertility, workplace conflict, loss...the list can go on and on. Those are heavy things to deal with, and no one should ever tell you not to feel emotions like sorrow, anger, or grief.

You are human. You struggle. It's okay, and sharing some of those struggles helps to make ourselves more human to our students. I'm convinced that some students believe we live at school. (Why else would they be so shocked when they see us buying toilet paper at the store?) Sharing a few of our struggles help us connect with them. They begin to see us as a human that can hopefully help them deal with their big issues. It always comes up that I struggle with depression and anxiety, and that I go to counseling for those things. I don't spill all the details, but just sharing that amount has opened doors for me to console kids who had anxiety and mini-panic attacks. Sharing a bit of how you struggle can be a good thing.

# *No one should ever tell you not to feel emotions like sorrow, anger, or grief.*

I don't want to give the wrong message either. "Shut Up and Teach" is not a call to toxic positivity. Toxic positivity is, basically, the belief that we should always be in a positive mindset and mood, even if life kind of sucks for us. Kendra Cherry, MS, states it pretty clearly: "Toxic positivity denies people the authentic support that they need to cope with what they are facing" (*Why Toxic Positivity Can be so Harmful*, 2021). In the same article, Cherry also claims that toxic positivity is dangerous because it shames and causes guilt, denies authentic human emotions, and prevents emotional growth. "Shut Up and Teach" is not about that. I'm not saying that you should never take a mental health day. I still take a few days each year to rest and recover emotionally and mentally.

If you are struggling and need some help, there are lots of resources. In the upcoming chapter "A Safe Place to Be," I offer some ideas for what to do when you are struggling. Mandy Froehlich (@froehlichm) offers mindfulness and SEL courses on her website (www.mandyfroehlich.com) for teachers who may be struggling in different areas of their job. One course in particular (Self-Care for Educators) focuses on physical, emotional, intellectual, and spiritual self-care, which is very beneficial when searching for balance in our lives. Whatever you are going through right now, there are resources that can provide you with what you need to get through it.

Now, with that said, I do not condone complaining without an intent to find a solution, spilling all the gory details about our struggles, teaching with a poor attitude, or teaching with practices that are not effective. It does no good. We have to shut our doors, shut our mouths, and teach. We must make school a place where students and staff love to be, but complaining does the exact opposite. It drives others away from us. No one wants to work with staff who complain the entire time about problems, especially when they fail to offer up any solutions.

I got a solution for that: shut up and teach.

## THE BACKSTORY.

We all have those days when we would rather be anywhere but our jobs. As rewarding as the teaching profession is, it takes its toll on the best of us. We can become exhausted from the daily grind of teaching. There are seasons within a school year that are especially taxing on our minds and bodies, e.g., from October 31 through the end of December. Even when things are going great, those moments where we feel like we just need a break are legitimate. Oh, have I mentioned the sick days? Those are the days (or at least before COVID-19 changed the world) when we show up to work anyway because it's more work to create sub plans and stay home with a sinus infection than it is to just power through it.

I have those days. I had one that drove me mad! I was dealing with my monsters (anxiety and depression), and it just so happened to fall in the middle of a season where it seemed like everything had to be done (grades, report cards, prepping for parent/teacher conferences). I wished more than anything for a snow day. Sure it was in the middle of October (it never snows in New Mexico during October...or hardly ever), but I was exhausted, mentally and physically, and I just didn't want to be there.

As I sat at my desk, about an hour or so before the kids arrived, I had a self-check: I need to snap out of this or go home. Obviously, going home wasn't an option, and that's when I mentally told myself the following: Shut up and teach, Elijah.

Shut up and teach. Something I needed to hear, and something that, perhaps, some of you need to hear. Teachers, the time is now to stop complaining and griping, and do our jobs. The passion and intention behind that phrase are not to diminish your problems, but to inspire you to leave behind any attitude that will negatively impact your ability to teach effectively.

## ONE SIDE OF THE COIN.

I once had a conversation with some students about December. I mentioned that December and even Christmas are kind of hard for me to get through. They asked why. I didn't spill all the details, but I gracefully explained that there are some painful memories attached to December, which makes it hard. One boy said, "You're usually very happy and hard-working. Does this mean that you're going to be lazy and sad during December?" The concern in his eyes was for both of us. He wanted me to feel okay, but I could tell he was legitimately concerned for his well-being. The question he asked without asking was this: *Will you be the teacher I need during December, or will you be the grouchy teacher no one wants?* I explained that they would have no idea when I was having a bad day. "You won't know when I'm having a rough day because I've already had rough days with you this year. You knew nothing about that because I refuse to bring my bad attitude and all my problems here."

That's what it means to shut up and teach. It's not ignoring your problems; it's leaving your problems in the car, or better yet, at home. Don't bring that negativity into the room. Your kids feed on this. I once worked with a teacher who complained about everything. I didn't care to collaborate with this teacher because it turned into such a whine festival. The only thing missing was the cheese.... Anyway, that year, like every year I worked there, we were tasked to observe different classrooms. I entered this teacher's room, and I could tell she brought that negative, complaining spirit into her room. Her kids complained about almost everything they had to do. There was no joy in the work being done. No one wanted to be there, most of all, her students.

On the other hand, I worked with a specials teacher who was really loved by the kids. She taught six classes a day. Her last class was at that time of the day when everyone needs a moment to themselves to either scream, cry, cuss, or just breathe. What's interesting, though, is that for some kids, her last class was the best part of their day. One time a student told her that she noticed that the teacher seemed happy to see them, even at the end of the day, and she wasn't grumpy, tired, and annoyed when they came to see her. She responded by telling them that they deserve a happy teacher, a teacher that will be energetic all day.

Now, that's how you shut up and teach!

**Stop and reflect: Have you experienced a time when your students picked up on your attitude? Was it positive or negative?**

If we are in the business of making school a place that kids love to be, then we have to shut up and teach. We can't expect that our kids will enjoy our classrooms when we don't even enjoy being there. That story at the beginning, when I told myself to get it together, turned out to be good! Oh, I addressed my attitude a little after the kids left; I still felt tired, and I still wanted to get home as quickly as I could, but my kids knew nothing of it. They didn't need to. It would've torn down the enthusiasm that we so desperately needed in our classroom. It would've taught my students that complaining is fine, even if no solutions are presented.

*We can't expect that our kids will enjoy our classrooms when we don't even enjoy being there.*

The other thing is that my attitude did actually change for the better that day. I wasn't just faking a good attitude for my kids. I began to see the good things going on: a student making progress, kindness among students, happy faces, engagement. When you shut up and teach, you will begin to see the good things happening because that's what you're focused on. When your focus is clouded by negativity, all you will see is the negative. By shutting up and teaching away, we begin to make school a place that we love to be, too.

We are human, and, yes, we complain. In the long run, though, venting and complaining do nothing to solve problems, whether those are personal or professional problems. They certainly have no place in our classrooms. Our energy influences our students' attitudes. What kind of attitude and outlook do we want them to have: one where they can't wait to leave or one where they can't wait to come back the next day?

## THE OTHER SIDE OF THE COIN.

The other side of the *Shut Up and Teach* coin is another call to action. It's a call to abandon all excuses for why we teach with outdated methods and, instead, to teach with passion, engagement, excitement, innovation, and pride.

I've already talked a lot about bringing passion, engagement, and fun into our classrooms. The days when I'm lacking those things are the days I need to be told to shut up and teach. On the days when I'm lacking the engagement and energy I need, shut up and teach comes to mind. It might sound different to everyone, but in my mind, this is what it sort of sounds like.

*Adding in a new element will transform this lesson into an experience. Although it's new to you, it's worth it for them. Shut up and teach.*

*Shut up and teach more than a worksheet.*

*Yes, you will look silly wearing this costume. Who cares? Your kids are in for an experience today. Shut up and teach.*

*Yes, this lesson requires a lot of prep, and you might have to get to school 30 minutes earlier than normal to set up. Your students deserve a sweet science lab experience. Shut up and teach.*

You see, it's not just about putting the bad attitude aside; it's also about putting the bad practices aside. I don't mean to keep beating a dead horse, but we have to find a way to make our teaching captivating, engaging, exciting, and memorable. We don't do that when we teach with outdated methods. Yes, it is easier to watch a Bill Nye video, but your kids can do that at home or on their own at school. They may not be able to look at rock types under a microscope at home. They can read about plants at home and in class, but some students live in environments without plants or vegetation. Take them outside to study the plants at school.

This side of the *Shut Up and Teach* coin is about taking teaching to the next level. We have to shut up when we start making excuses for why we can't do something really big and fun. We have to tell the voice saying, "But that's the way I've always done this," to shut up. We have to shut up and teach with passion, excitement, and engagement.

**Stop and reflect: When have you had a Shut Up and Teach moment? What lesson(s) did you learn from the experience?**

———

Let's make school a place that students love to be. Bring excitement and passion back to your classroom. Leave that bad attitude behind. Tell the outdated practices to shut up. Bring your experiences and engagement to your students.

Shut up and teach.

———

*From Tracey Taylor - Art Teacher, Artist, Entrepreneur*

There is a strange transformation that happens to me when I step into a classroom at school, and it has happened for as long as I can remember. The first person to recognize it was a close teacher friend of my mother. I was in college working on acquiring my observation hours at the very beginning of my journey to become a certified educator. At that time in my life, I was struggling, as many young adults do...with carving my identity, my path, my direction, my life, basically. After a few rounds of observation and work in that second-grade classroom, my mother's friend told my mother, "... if we can just get her to graduate, she is going to be one excellent teacher." I believe to this day that she was the first to witness this whole transformation situation that occurs...when I shut up and teach.

As a little kid, I was always excited to watch Disney movies and especially the television program *The Wonderful World of Disney*. I'm not sure if it was the time of day the program aired or the presentation of the content, but there was always a particular internal buzz that filled my bucket to the brim on those Sunday afternoons/evenings when I got to watch Tinkerbell fairy dust

Cinderella's castle and then bring magic, merriment, and the spirit of creativity through that screen. Interestingly to note, Sunday afternoon/evening time at around 4 or 5 is still my favorite time and day...as a photographer and artist, there's something truly special about the quality of light during that time that I appreciate very much. The atmosphere seems different in its suspension around me, as if it feeds and recharges my heart, soul, and mind for the upcoming week. That has become a sacred space for me for sure. All these years later, it is during this time each week, I typically spend time thinking about my upcoming week; some would call this casting vision; it is certainly reflective, whatever you call it...What is on my calendar? What are my priorities? What are my big checkmark moments? (Shout out to my fellow bullet journal peeps!) What do I have? What do I need? I hear you asking the question, "T, do you mean to tell us that you spend an hour or more meditating on each week you teach?" Um, yeah...I do. I also spend time each morning focusing on just the day at hand. And, what's more, if I don't get that time in, I feel disorganized and unfocused, as if I am working without fences. As an artistic mind and a person of creativity, I find it a necessity to be mindful of organization and linear daily function, for without, I will end up following a white rabbit down a hole or chasing an inky butterfly around to my heart's desire. That open range can be a bit disastrous when it comes to deadlines. Confession....I can be a bit "ride or die" when it comes to a routine because I truly need them for functioning structure.

I rarely walk into a classroom not having a secure mind about the business at hand and the goals for the day and week anymore. I have certainly had my fair share of days where, at times, I was flying by the seat of my pants and pulling a rabbit out of my hat in less than a few seconds. Inevitably though, I always end up thinking to myself that I should have taken the time to be mindful and prepared, so to avoid the drama inside my head, I prepare. The first few years of my teaching career, I maintained a professional development plan that focused on time management, organization, development of content, and assessment of learning. I needed that. Now with almost twenty years backing me, those four things are still my main focus each year, each topic, each lesson, each class. Remember me saying just moments ago that I was a bit "ride or die" when it comes to a routine? This time management, organization, content, and assessment plan is my cause and cure and my default when it comes to the grind. If any of those four pieces are off or misaligned, I feel what we commonly refer to as stress. And now, as a veteran educator, it doesn't typically take much to get everything back into place and running smoothly because I just have to sit down, analyze, deconstruct, and reassemble whichever piece it is that is maladjusted. In all transparency, it can be taxing to work weekly and daily at keeping those pieces in order. Thankfully, they are also the support scaffolding for when I am fatigued, distracted, or simply not feeling it. I lean heavily on having those four pieces secured, even if everything else is melting down around me.

As a kid, I remember my Momma often saying that everything has a space and everything needs to be in its place. Somehow, I must have taken this to heart on a grand scale, not just when it came time to clean up a mess of epic proportion. Once I am satisfied that all four pieces of my preparation for my classroom are in place, I feel secure enough that I can have students walk into my room. The minute I open the door to my classroom to greet students is hour zero. Everything up to that minute is prep time. Once that zero minute hits, it is school time. It is time to shut up and teach. Tinkerbell has sprinkled her fairy dust over the castle, and it's time to make the magic of learning happen.

It is an absolute joy to be around new teachers, fresh out of college, with their energy and enthusiasm for everything school. I also make it a point to have conversations with students about what they dislike or hate about the process of school. What is it about school that you loved as a kid? Did you ever have that moment of hating school or thinking that you as a student could do a better job of teaching a subject better than the current instructor? Do you remember the feel of the desk or the classroom environment? Reflecting on these things helps keep me up the supply of fairy dust and magic. It is why I chose to become a teacher in the first place.

I grew up in schools. Both of my parents are teachers, my twin brothers are both teachers, my brothers are both married to teachers....either we are amid a generational curse, or we are legacy living. Regardless, dinner at our house should count for college credit. The folks my parents chose to spend their time with outside of work were so often other teachers. So, schools and the people who made and worked in the school world were safe places for me. Growing up part of a community with such an amazing cast of characters has given me a plethora of great heroes, good examples, and some "learning what not to do" moments in which to expand as I endeavor in my craft. I am the sum of all those teachers pouring into me over the years. And what I didn't get from them, I ventured to gain for myself. You see, at some point in my struggle, I had to sort out how I learned things. Gosh! Once I learned how to acquire knowledge for myself, I felt like I had gained a superpower. And when I open the door to my classroom in that zero hour-minute, I am ready, willing, and able to help students get to that same point...where they can gain their powers to learn, to navigate, to think, to be better prepared for a time that we all know is coming...the day when they will have to carve out their own identity, destination, the path of their life's journey. When I have truly done what I needed to do to prepare for that zero hour-minute, and the door opens, the students enter, and just like magic, POOF! I am the very best version of myself. Those of you who know me personally understand that in my private world or home life, I run on a pretty strong combination of caffeine, nicotine, Jesus, and cuss words. But, when that magic takes over...watch out! I am a princess: lovely, patient, and kind. I am the villain, playing Devil's advocate, asking tough questions, and making lazy brains think from a different perspective. I am the hero saving the day when mistakes threaten a growth mindset. I am the funny, friendly character laughing at jokes, telling stories of how I used to get in trouble in school, and always has a band-aid if you need one. I am an astronaut daring to dream big dreams and quite possibly speaking different languages. I am Ms. Hodges' loud as life laugh and piano from the back of the room, Mrs. Shannon's social studies stories, Mr. Newman's music, Mr. Allen's handwriting, and Miss McDonald's avocado tasting. I am Eugene and Myrna's daughter; and Kevin and Kerry's little sister. I am all that and MORE...now that is a four-letter word that can cause some real controversy.

What will you bring and share with them in the short time in which they are your students? My very first principal used to tell us from the time that door opens to the time that it closes, you are theirs. Be there in a way that meets their needs. I still maintain that ethic today. That paperwork, those union issues, that meeting or memo that has you twisted, home stuff, health stuff, find a space and place for it. It needs your effort and honesty too, but not while you have kids wanting, waiting, watching for magic.

# CHAPTER 10
# ROCK THE MIC

M usic speaks to me. For me, those cliche sayings, "Music is what emotions sound like," and, "When words fail, music speaks," really fit. Punk rock music holds a special place in my heart. I enjoy listening to bands like The Suicide Machines, Sum 41, Fall Out Boy, The Offspring, All Time Low, Black Flag, Weezer, Bad Religion, and my all-time favorite pop-punk band, Green Day.

I'll never forget the first time I heard Green Day's iconic "American Idiot" album. I was captivated and drawn into the message they were so passionate about. Songs like "Are We the Waiting" and "Letterbomb" have so much sincerity and passion behind them.

I've had the chance to see Green Day in concert, once during their Revolution Radio tour, and again during the Hella Mega Tour with Fall Out Boy and Weezer. Oh. My. Goodness. The energy there was infectious! It's amazing to hear an entire amphitheater scream out "Amen!" right when Billie Joe Armstrong holds out the mic, signaling that it's our time to join him in singing "Holiday." He drove the entire audience insane when, right after the killer solo on "Know Your Enemy," he said, "I need someone who knows the lyrics to come up here and sing!" The pure joy from that guy who helped Green Day finish the song! It was awesome.

Rockstars love to do this. They get the audience to participate with them by really listening to the audience and encouraging them to sing with them. They want the energy to take over the audience. If the energy is only circling the band on stage, then what's the point of having an audience, right? Besides that, the energy only magnifies when it's shared between the band and the audience. It's that energy that is shared between the band and the audience that makes rock shows so much fun. Don't believe me? Rewatch Queen's performance at Live Aid to see how Freddie Mercury got the audience to participate with them.

Going to a symphony or an orchestra can be enjoyable, but you won't have that same infectious energy from a rock concert. That's why I don't always prefer to attend a symphony: there's no audience participation. The crowd is not involved. I went a few times in college for a music appreciation class I was taking, and was told by my instructor to hold back my applause until someone else started to clap. "You don't want to clap at the wrong time. You'll look out of place and look a little foolish."

I can't help but wonder what kind of "shows" our students attend. Are we rock stars letting our audience (students) rock the mic with us? Or are we the classical music composer waiting for our audience to be impressed with our skills once our song (lesson) is over? If we aren't letting our students rock the mic, why not? Why won't we give them the stage and let them lead the class?

**Stop and reflect: How do we encourage the "symphony" teacher to break free and become the "rockstar" teacher?**

## LOSS OF CONTROL.

For some teachers, based on what I've seen and been told, it's too difficult to let go of control. Those teachers wrote a symphony that needs to be played note for note. There can be no mistakes. There can't be any interruptions or improvising. These teachers don't empower their students to be active participants, but, instead, they expect them to be audience members that sit still, shut up, and do their work.

But what I love about Green Day is that they don't sound exactly like their recordings. They add measures during some instrumental parts. They play songs like "American Idiot" and "Hitchin' a Ride" a little differently to include more audience participation. It's okay if it's not exactly the way it was written; they are creating an experience that the crowd will never forget. What experiences are we creating by allowing ourselves to improvise and let our students participate in the teaching? Will they go home thinking, "Wow, my teacher is talented," or will they go home thinking, "I can't believe I got to lead the class today"? The second is more memorable and impactful. Let them rock the mic!

## IT'S OKAY IF THEY "MESS UP."

Another reason we fail to let kids rock the mic is that, well, we don't want them to mess up. This is true for me, anyway. The times I hold back are when I'm doubting my students' abilities to lead. (How messed up is that, right?) That doubt wasn't to be found in Billie Joe Armstrong. He called a girl up to play guitar for a song. (She even got to keep the guitar. Lucky!) But what's interesting is that he had to teach her the song. She messed up the timing once or twice, and she had a difficult time figuring out the chord progression.

Now, if this happened in some classrooms, some teachers would immediately tell the girl to sit back down and allow them to demonstrate how it was done, adding in a polite but backhanded, "Don't worry, you'll get it next time. Nice try." Not Billie Joe Armstrong. He stayed right next to her, teaching her while the rest of the band grooved and played patiently while she figured it out, which eventually she did. (Did I mention that she got to keep the guitar after all that? So cool!)

We need to have that same mentality. We know that when we let our kids lead the class that things might not go smoothly. They will make mistakes, they will stumble a bit, they may give false information, and they may forget everything that they know when they stand up in front of everyone. That's okay! We need to let our kids make mistakes. It's one way that they learn. You and your other students can respectfully help them correct the mistake and find their place again. Besides, they'll learn from that mistake and the in-the-moment teaching that you will provide. Remember, that girl left with a guitar and a new song she had learned.

Our kids will learn when we give them control and let them rock the mic.

## *LET THEM LEAD WITH HARD WORK.*

We need to let our students rock the mic for another reason: letting the kids rock the mic will create leaders, not just followers. It's one thing to give a killer lesson, but it's another to let the kids lead a killer lesson. The impact goes further than if you are the only one teaching. I told you that I once dressed up as Blackbeard when I taught biographies. I spent the whole day dressed as a pirate, talking to them as if I was Blackbeard, giving them my story, "captured and held them captive" on Queen Anne's Revenge. When it was over, the kids got excited because I told them it was their turn to lead. They were given a similar task: dress up as a famous individual who they admired (if they wanted to) and report on that important and inspirational figure in the first person.

*They put in the work, because I passed the mic to them for a bit.*

And they did! They presented as if they were that individual. My fourth-grade students came dressed as Walt Disney, Simone Biles, Johnny Cash, and more significant people. The students presented to their classmates and led the classroom in quality learning. It wasn't just the dressing up and presentation, though. It took hours of research using multiple sources of information. It took time to decide on and put together a costume. It became fun and exciting for them, but it took work. They put in the work because I passed the mic to them for a bit.

**Stop and reflect: What valuable lessons have you learned from letting your kids rock the mic?**

———————

That's what it means to let kids rock the mic. It's letting them work hard, struggle a bit, and allow their voices to be heard. Some of my favorite moments in the classroom are when I can step back and watch my kids discuss something they read or the best way to solve a word problem. I can step back and see students passing the mic back and forth, leading the class. That should be every educator's goal: to see our students become leaders, to see them participate in the teaching, not just the learning.

So let's pass that mic off to that student in your classroom. Let them lead and participate. Let go of some of the control in your room. Let them make mistakes, but don't ever take the mic out of their hands.

---

*From Joshua Buckley, Elementary Assistant Principal, Mesa, AZ, Co-Host of the Punk Rock Classrooms Podcast (@joshrbuckley / @punkclassrooms)*

Share the stage. Share the mic.

I grew up in the punk scene. Most weekends in high school I was either on stage jumping around, playing guitar or I was in the crowd singing...well, more likely shouting along to the songs. One of the great things about the small shows I went to, the community we built in those halls and basements, was how we all had the shared experience of the "show." Whether you were on the stage or in the crowd, you were part of it. Oftentimes that line between them blurred when a singer on stage would stick the mic into the crowd and welcome the audience to sing along, to be a part of the action, or better yet, the crowd was welcomed on stage to sing along and be a part of it all. On Mondays, after those weekends on the stage or in the crowd, I would come back to school and come back to a classroom where the mic wasn't handed over to the crowd. There was no "sing-along" with the crowd. Most periods, it was the teacher's show, and we were just there to watch.

When I became a classroom teacher, I wanted to change that. I wanted to share the mic and the stage with my students. I wanted them to make my room more like those basement venues and VFW halls where I was able to move and sing along. I tried my best to give opportunities for their learning to be shared, loud, and moving. Whether it was having students write songs about the Salem Witch Trials to share with the class, having them create a nightly news segment they acted out about events in the Revolutionary War, or having them design their own way to showcase what we just learned in class, I wanted them to "rock the mic." I wanted them to feel a part of the show and not a passive viewer of the learning in class.

It's not always easy to give up control of our classrooms. Sometimes the songs are off key, and sometimes the mosh pit gets out of hand, but that's part of the learning process, for the students and for us. It's gonna be messy sometimes, and it's not always gonna be perfect. As educators, if we want students to own their learning, we need to guide and facilitate. We set boundaries, set up parameters for success, and give them the tools they need to take the stage. The best part is when you've done your job as the facilitator; when you have set them up for success, you can take a step back and let them run with the learning in your classroom. Once you've done that, they can truly "rock the mic." They can have that basement show experience. They can jump from the crowd to the stage and every-where in between and own their learning.

## CHAPTER 11
# A SAFE PLACE TO BE

Q uestion: is the responsibility of healing from trauma entirely up to the individual?

Follow-up question: If you feel you are never fully healed from your trauma, is it your fault?

Some might argue that it is, in fact, your fault if you never fully heal from your trauma. However, in an article written by Brian Peck, LCSW, he dispels this myth that not being healed is your fault. Peck says:

"Your responsibility" also comes across to many survivors as "why aren't you trying harder," or implies survivors have chosen to remain stuck in trauma. These sentiments, while well-meaning, don't fully grasp how trauma works and are often fueled by the toxic positivity permeating our society...Telling someone who is in freeze/collapse physiology that they are responsible for their own healing can make a dark and lonely place even more isolating. In many ways, this approach reinforces the experience of powerlessness...Supporting survivors' physiological need for safety, power, and connection can create a context for healing. Expecting survivors to live up to the social construct of rugged individualism will likely not be helpful for many survivors. (Peck, *What You Should Know Before Sharing This 'Inspirational' Trauma Meme*, 2019)

It's reasonable to say that you should do something to try and heal: go to counseling, meditate, pray, or (and only if prescribed and managed by your personal doctor) take medication to help you. However, trauma finds a way to linger. Take it from me: trauma sucks, and it's not your fault if your trauma still rears its ugly head now and then.

Some of our students have real trauma. I have taught students who have witnessed domestic violence and lived out of the backseat of a car; a student whose house was shot up by a gang while they were home; students who have been neglected and abandoned by their parents; a student whose mom was killed in a car accident in the middle of the school year; students who watched their father get arrested for driving under the influence while the students were in the car.

Sometimes, students bring their trauma to school. Some have learned to cope, but it can still impact many areas of the child's life. It's our job to make school a place that students love to be, even with their trauma. Students need a safe place to learn. If school is going to be a place that students love to be, that means educators need to do everything in their power to make school a safe place.

One of the things that I tell students is that I want them to feel safe and comfortable in the classroom. Our class usually discusses what that would look like, sound like, and feel like, but there are also some things I do personally, because I've seen the impact that they have on students. Here are some of the things I proactively do to make my students feel as safe as possible.

## ADDRESS EVERY STUDENT.

I talked about this in a previous chapter, but addressing the students you pass by or see throughout the day shows them that they are noticed and welcomed at your school. Can you imagine going a whole day at work without being addressed? Not even a "hello"? Those little things can help students feel welcomed at your school. They make them feel a little more at ease.

In the book *Kids Deserve It*, Adam Welcome and Todd Nesloney say that "...it's an honor to talk with kids and listen to them..." (2016). I believe this is true. Whether it is during class or just in passing, students should feel welcome at school. A simple "hello" can go such a long way to making students feel welcome and safe at school.

## DO YOUR VERY BEST NOT TO YELL AT A STUDENT.

I will be the first one to admit that I am guilty of this. There are times when a student has pressed my buttons, and I just lost my cool with them. I have gotten into a screaming match with some kids. I cringe when I think about what sort of trauma I either created for that student or the emotions that I triggered by yelling at that student. Teachers: stop yelling at your kids. I don't care who you are, what your teaching style is, or what the student has done. Screaming at kids is doing nothing to make that student feel safe. It escalates the situation and frustrates the student even more. (Plus, I have discovered that some students just get too much pleasure out of watching me yell, making what I am yelling about extremely ineffective.) Just stop yelling at your students, please.

## NEVER HUMILIATE A STUDENT.

Again, I'll be the first to admit that I've done this. I've shamed students in front of their peers, and it devastates me to think about what kind of damage I did to that kid over something that was probably insignificant. There's always a little room for sarcasm, but never at the expense of embarrassing a student. That student may be shamed and humiliated on a daily basis by their family. You need to be the safe person that they want to be with, not another person who adds to their trauma.

## MAKE YOUR CLASSROOM SAFE.

Let kids know the procedures for events like fire drills, shelter-in-place, and lockdowns; it puts their minds at ease knowing that the adult in the room has a safety plan in place. Some teachers keep things like water and food in their closets for those kids who may only eat when they come to school. Don't tolerate bullying of any kind. Don't allow kids to have their way with other kids. Set firm expectations for behavior and make it clear that bullying and being intentionally mean won't be allowed because you are striving to make your classroom a safe place for everyone.

School should be a place where students love to be. They should be eager to get to our classrooms, not only because we make learning exciting, but because we make them feel safe. Our classes should be a safe place where students feel comfortable expressing their voice, sharing their culture, identifying who they are, and celebrating the differences that make everyone unique. Don't tolerate bullying of any kind, especially when the bullying is aimed at another student's race, ethnicity, gender, sexual orientation, language, religion, and other parts of a student's culture. Work hard to model and create an environment of respect towards each other.

> *Everyone in the class is important, every voice matters, and everyone is safe under our vision.*

In my classroom, we create a vision. The vision has a list of what we want more and less of in our classroom and across our entire school. The vision isn't necessarily a list of rules or "do's and don'ts," but a guide for how we should treat each other, ourselves, and our materials. I don't write it out and tell them what the vision is either. It is created on day one by the students and myself, but mostly by the students. It's their vision of what makes school great and safe, and it includes *everyone's* voice. Everyone has a chance to share what they want. When students see, talk about, or add new things to the vision (a reminder that your anchor charts should serve as living documents, not just decorations), it serves to remind them that everyone in the class is important, every voice matters, and everyone is safe under our vision.

Another thing to consider when striving to be safe is to avoid triggering attention getters. I don't flick the lights on and off, because I have taught students who were afraid of the dark and would get anxious if the lights were off. And it's not just younger students. See, fear of the dark isn't just being scared of darkness. According to Sarah Lewis, PharmD:

Sometimes, people can link their fear of the dark to a specific negative experience. In this case, the fear involves an area of the brain called the amygdala. This tiny region records reactions to experiences. When something particularly scary occurs in the dark, the amygdala remembers it. Then, it reminds you of the scariness when you encounter darkness or a similar situation. (*Achluophobia (Fear of the Dark): Causes, Symptoms & Treatments*, 2020)

Lewis also states that, "Children who fear the dark may withdraw from peers due to shame about the fear. This can lead to loneliness and even academic problems" (2020). That's all the evidence I need to avoid things like flicking the lights on and off to get their attention.

I used to, but have stopped, clapping to get kids' attention. (This is the classic teacher claps and the students echo the clap back method.) Clapping unexpectedly is triggering to students who have suffered physical abuse, like slapping. I know because a student told me so. Clapping, when the student was aware that clapping was about to take place, was okay; however, a sudden and unexpected clap reminded the student of some of the physical abuse they had suffered. A lot of schools strive to have a hand signal to get students' attention silently, which is perfect. It gives students a chance to self-regulate and focus while you get their attention in a peaceful way.

**Stop and reflect: What are you doing or can you do to make your school and classroom safe?**

## ADDRESS YOUR OWN TRAUMA.

Teachers have trauma too. Some teachers reading this may be dealing with sickness, death, previous (or current) toxic work environments, divorce, addictions, exhaustion, domestic violence...the list could go on. We owe it to ourselves to be better for our children. Take a personal, self-care day. Go work out. Exercise your faith (if you hold one).

One of the best decisions I ever made was to start going to counseling on a regular basis and begin medication for my anxiety and depression. It helped me sort through the things I couldn't sort through on my own. It made me more focused, helped me think straighter, and live with a sense of peace. In the long run, I became a better teacher because I was in a better mental state. Please, do what you need to in order to take care of yourself.

**Stop and reflect: What are you doing to take care of yourself? Identify one thing you can start doing today to help yourself.**

---

It's going to take a lot to keep our kids safe and comfortable at school. It's not easy, and it's not listed in the job description. Protecting, even if it means putting your life on the line, is not something that they prepare you for in college. Everyone who works with students in any capacity has the role of creating a safe place for students. We have the greatest profession in the world, and with that comes the greatest responsibility: to care for another human being—young human beings, who, unfortunately, have to sometimes deal with very big problems. Although their trauma may linger throughout their life, we are always present. We are always there to care for them and love them through the darkest times. Our voices will be with them. Their memories of how kind and supportive we were may just save them. They may not remember your math lessons, but they will remember how you made them feel important and cared for. They won't remember all the stories you read, but they will carry the memory of your laughter and smile, and how you always made them feel safe. Don't underestimate just how large of an impact you can and will make when your students feel safe with you.

# CHAPTER 12
# THE MARIGOLD

This is a chapter about one of my tattoos and my favorite flower.

Oh, and education, of course.

Tattoos are meaningful to me. I don't get random tattoos. Each one holds a special place in my heart and has a deep meaning behind it. My spartan helmet represents brotherhood. (Most of my brothers also have spartan helmet tattoos.) The broken lightbulb with a rose is a symbol of my mental health journey. Even the word "Stank" tattooed on my foot is there for an important reason.

I have 12 tattoos currently. One of the more recent tattoos I got is a pirate flag. (It's a pirate's life for me!) My idea for this tattoo came to life with the help of Tracey Taylor (a working artist, art teacher, my mentor, and my wife...she's pretty rad at all those things, by the way!), and Jesse Williamson (one of my badass tattoo artists in Farmington, NM). It was really cool to take the idea of what I wanted and to see it come to life through the work of other artists.

(The pirate flag of The Marigold, created by Tracey Taylor and Jesse Williamson.)

The pirate flag was the first tattoo I got that represented teaching. I do my best to stick to the PIRATE code laid out in the *Like a PIRATE* books by Dave Burgess Consulting Inc. I strive to teach my heart out and to teach with excellence. The skull on that flag reminds me to do that.

## GUIDANCE AND SUPPORT.

On the flag are two purple marigolds. Marigolds are beautiful flowers, or at least I think so. I love that they are used during Dia de Los Muertos (The Day of the Dead). For anyone who is unfamiliar with Dia de Los Muertos, it is a Mexican holiday where the living honor their deceased ancestors in various ways, such as leaving food, pictures, flowers, and other valuables on the graves of their ancestors. At home, an ofrenda (offering table) with pictures of the ancestors is set up. Marigolds are used to help lure the spirits of the dead back to the land of the living.

This brings me to my first point: we should strive to be the marigold with the purpose of guiding others to where they are headed. As teachers, we should be guiding our students to discover their passions and identities. We should help them discover who they are. We do this by introducing them to new content, reading quality literature to them, making connections with them on a daily basis, giving them experiences and not just lessons, and teaching them with passion and energy. Like a marigold guiding the spirits to the land of the living, we should be guiding students into their possibilities: drama teachers, scientists, coders, activists, business leaders, farmers, plumbers, electricians, politicians, contractors, tattoo artists, musicians, police officers, airline pilots...all possibilities that we, the marigolds, should be guiding them to.

*We should be guiding students into their possibilities.*

Secondly, marigolds are great companion flowers. According to an article I read online, when marigolds are planted with other flowers and plants, marigolds can actually help keep certain pests away, therefore saving the other plants (Seleshanko, n.d.). So, in a huge way, marigolds support other plants in their growth. Are we marigolds supporting our fellow teachers and students? I hope we're not the pests tearing each other apart. We need to be able to help everyone around us grow to their full potential. Regardless of how many years we have been teaching or in the type of schools we have taught in, I believe that everyone has something to share to make the person next to them better. We all have something to give to our students and ways to help them grow. Whether it's giving our kids the courage to take risks, imparting knowledge and strategies for solving problems, modeling how to resolve conflict with others, being there for them in their time of crisis, supporting their dreams, cheering them on at their games, encouraging kids to find their identity and self-worth...all those things help build our children up. They help them grow as individuals and students. And when we do that, we create a place they love.

## PRIDE AND SUCCESS.

Why purple, though? After all, orange marigolds are used during Dia de Los Muertos. Well, I found out that purple flowers actually symbolize success. Success should be something that every teacher and student aims for. We need to aim for success through hard work and a healthy amount of pride in that work. Teachers: don't half-ass your job. We have the greatest profession in the world because we, as marigolds, open the doors of all other professions to our kids. When we do our best and take pride in our work, we make our classroom a place that is enjoyable and where our students can learn and grow.

## We are in the business of making school a place that students love.

And here is where success comes in. Only through hard work and pride will everyone—students and teachers—find true success. We are in the business of making school a place that students love, which means they need to be successful. They, too, need to feel pride and success in their work. When we pour into them, when we become the marigold for our students, then they too can become successful, work hard, and take pride in their efforts.

**Stop and reflect: In what ways do you model pride and success daily to your students?**

---

Guidance, support, pride, and success. Everything that comes after these is important, but I believe that if we miss these things, then we are just robots programming other robots. But here is the thing: we aren't robots, and we aren't *just* teachers; we are support for our kids, a guiding light, and a model of hard work and success.

So who wants to sail on my ship, The Marigold? Who wants to help others by being a guide and support? Who wants to make pride and success through hard work their mission? I hope that you will join me. The schoolhouse only becomes a place where students and teachers want to be when we become the great companion flower that helps make the soil richer and the plants in it grow to their full potential.

Stop and reflect: Who is your marigold? A principal? A family member? Co-worker? Give them a shout-out in person (call, text, email, etc.) or on social media.

## CHAPTER 13
# LET'S TALK RELATIONSHIPS

P arent/teacher conferences had just finished a couple of days before I started to write this chapter. I decided that the students would lead most of the conference. They completed a quick reflection survey, explaining how things were going for them. Some of the questions included, "What is one goal you have for the next quarter of the year?" and "What is one achievement that you are proud of?"

I sat across the table, listening to students explain to their families all the things that they are proud of, what they need to work on, how their behavior was for the last quarter and their goals for ELA and math. I was excited to hear a lot of thoughtful ideas about how they could reach their goals. I was also excited to hear that students were happy that I incorporated the Grid Method into math and reading. Some students were really happy that we had science class every day.

One boy said that the thing he was most proud of was that he isn't as shy anymore and that he had made friends. It got me thinking about overlooked aspects of going to school, one of which is the relationships that students build with teachers and other students. Relationships aren't just a buzzword in the world of education. Strong and wise educators know that relationships come first. We are in the business of teaching other human beings, not just programming mindless drones. We are in the business of educating the whole child.

Don't believe me? Why do you think having substitute teachers is stressful? No offense to substitute teachers, but it's just not the same when the teacher is gone. A sub is walking into a classroom to teach students that they (sometimes) don't know, with procedures and a schedule that is unfamiliar to them. They have to work very hard to manage students—all students: the compliant, the defiant, the ones with special needs, the shy, the loud, the ones who will push your buttons on a minute-by-minute basis, the ones who just lost a loved one, the one who missed four days in a row and needs to get caught up... need I go on?

Substitutes have their work cut out for them, not because they are incompetent, but because they don't have the relationship with the kids that the homeroom teacher has. Any teacher who does not have a positive relationship with their students is running uphill with a 50-pound pack on their back.

Storytime!

It was my fourth year of teaching. I had just moved to Aztec, New Mexico, and was teaching 29 fourth graders. I had some students who really challenged me, liked to push buttons, and had trouble regulating behaviors. I felt like I was running crowd control with a dash of teaching when I could get them settled down. By November, two of my students were placed in the Transition Room (a behavioral intervention classroom) full-time. By the end of the year, two more students were transferred into that class. I couldn't get my class to work for anything. Unfortunately, I turned into that teacher who yelled at their kids. The school was not the place that they wanted to be. It sucked. I had no idea what to do to motivate them. The work I managed to get them to turn in was poor quality, and every day seemed to get worse. I literally couldn't wait for the bell to ring. I started counting down days...in December. It was bad.

After that year ended, I thought long and hard about whether I was even going to return to teaching. Things had been so challenging that I had that *Am I really cut out to be a teacher?* moment. I decided that if I was to return that things needed to be different. My classroom needed to be calm, it needed to be a safe place for students, and it needed to be fun. But how?

How would I make this happen? I decided that I was going to focus on building relationships with kids.

## BECAUSE WE CARE ENOUGH.

In the past, I would allow kids to eat lunch with me *if* they had earned it with good behavior. It was during my fifth year of teaching (right after the really challenging year) that I started eating lunch with all the kids. Not every day, but at least a couple of times a week. I started doing this because I realized spending time with kids outside of the classroom was so important. It was necessary in order to build relationships with them. What better way to get to know others than around the table eating food, sharing stories, and laughing together? The big change from the previous year was that I removed the conditions and stopped being exclusive. I ate with them because I wanted to, and I ate with everyone.

I also started playing with them during recess. I would join them during a game of kickball. I played tetherball, four square, and played catch with my baseball kids. I'd record the time of kids who wanted to race each other. I'd race the students myself. Recess became a time for me to connect with students. It became a time to get to know them and for them to get to know me.

*I removed the conditions and stopped being exclusive.*

What else? I began to attend their events outside of school. In the past, I would attend one game out of obligation, but now it was because I genuinely cared about my students. I'd sit with their families during basketball and baseball games, so now I was also making connections with families. You learn a lot about who a child is when you sit next to their mom during a volleyball game. At the end of the game, I'd spend a brief moment to tell the students how proud of them I was. The amazing thing is the next day, I had more requests to attend their games.

You remember that old saying of people not caring about what you know until they know that you care. It's true. Students need to know that you care about who they are as a person, a student, an athlete, a gamer, a dancer. Whatever it is that they do, they want to know that you care about that part of their life. Not very many adults want to talk to you about what their top three favorite dinosaurs are, but kids tell us stuff like that because they want to know that we care, and as teachers, we do care. We care enough to spend time with them during unstructured moments like recess. We care enough to eat lunch with them and talk about everything but school. We care enough to ask questions, laugh with them, and build relationships.

When we talk about relationships, it shouldn't just be a buzzword. Building relationships shouldn't be another checkbox. "Oh, I went to my one required soccer game for the year. Now we have a solid relationship." Yeah?...no.

It's our job to educate students, to make school a place they love to be, and to impact human life. I believe developing healthy relationships with students is one of the best ways to do this. Students will work harder for the teacher who has invested in their lives than the teacher who demands that they follow directions. Just saying.

**Stop and reflect: What active steps are you currently taking to build positive relationships with your students?**

## PURE INTENTIONS MATTER.

I also feel it is important to make sure that our intentions are pure. Yes, building relationships is crucial and will go a long way to building positive school culture. However, kids are smart and can sense when we are being fake. They can sense when we are with them out of obligation or when we have some other impure intent, like treating positive relationships like it's a magic pill for all our problems. I have built really solid relationships with kids who still had lots of trouble regulating their behavior, getting work done, and getting along with others. Building a relationship with students won't solve all of your problems, and that's why it's important to check your intentions. Is it because you really care about them? Are you really interested in going to their game because you care about their interests outside of school?

When you are striving to build relationships with students, be authentic. Some of the students we teach don't trust adults because of the trauma and disappointment that they have experienced with the adults who should have been there for them. They know what it's like for an adult to say one thing and do another. They know what it's like for teachers to say one thing and do another. We have to check ourselves to see if there is any impure or insincere motive for building solid relationships with students. Be real. Be honest. Be pure. Work on those relationships because we're human beings desiring human connection. Do it because students deserve to have a trustworthy adult in their corner. Do it because it's the right thing to do.

---

One more quick story. I was walking back to my classroom with my students. We were outside for a science investigation and were coming back inside to get ready for lunch. A student looked at me and said, "Mr. C., do you, like, build relationships with kids because you think it's important?" When I told him yes (very important), he said, "I can tell that you like to do that with your students." They are watching and paying attention. I can't encourage this enough: build those relationships.

# CHAPTER 14
# GIVE THEM AN EXPERIENCE

*Me: Okay, everybody, today for our science lesson, we will be going outside to—*

*Student: Are we going outside to see science?*

This was an interaction I had with a student. In the past, kids have always been excited to go outside for any lesson that I've done outside. During my sixth year of teaching, I stepped up and took them outside more than ever.

We experienced friction on the blacktop and not so much friction on the wet grass. (That experience was funny!) We challenged ourselves to see who could melt a snowball the fastest. We have had the opportunity to go outside after heavy rain to see where the water goes and what it takes with it. We've completed sound surveys, and we melted ice cubes on colored paper.

Becky Schnekser (@schnekser) is a teacher who I have to thank right now for this. Becky is a teacher/scientist, and she teaches extremely well. In fact, she teaches her butt off! If I end up being half the science teacher that she is, I would be honored. She has taught me an important lesson:

science needs to be experienced. At the 2019 Teach Better Conference, she made a comment that we should be creating explorers, not encyclopedias. A mind-blowing statement! How often are we giving students the chance to explore and give them experiences rather than a mere lesson?

**Stop and reflect: What was an experience you had in school that was unforgettable?**

## EXPERIENCES TRUMP LESSONS.

That conversation with the student at the beginning of this chapter took place the day after a really cool lesson about weather, erosion, and deposition. We did some exploration of these concepts. I set up the science lab with tubs of sand. The kids made landforms, like mountains and canyons. Then they were told to blow (gently and not into others' faces) on their landforms. They wrote down their observations. They repeated the process, only this time they used a water dropper to represent rain. Once more, this time with a spray bottle to represent a river.

Science in action! This was an experience that helped them solidify the concepts being discussed in class. We followed it up the next day by going outside to complete an erosion observation. Armed with their notebooks and pencils, the students recorded objects that had experienced erosion and their locations. More science in action! Another chance to make a concept come to life and, like the girl told me, see science. It was an experience.

A couple of days later, my class went on a field trip. We went snowshoeing in Durango, Colorado, to learn about winter science, animal adaptations, and tips for surviving and thriving in winter. On the way there, a student had this conversation with me.

*Student: Mr. C., it looks like a giant took a chainsaw and chopped the mountain in half.*

*Me: Sure does. How do you think it really happened?*

*Student: Erosion. Probably wind or water.*

This brings up a good point: experiences stick with kids! Sure it was only a couple of days ago, so erosion was probably still fresh in her mind, but my students from previous years still recall experiences, like the snow-shoe field trip. Why? Because experiences are fun, impactful, and memorable.

We have to find as many ways as possible to give kids meaningful experiences during their time with us. School needs to be the place that they love to be. Sorry, but worksheets and lectures don't do that. Experiences will. Experiences are what students need. They make learning fun and real. It's no longer textbooks and YouTube videos. Yes, those have their place, but they aren't the end-all.

## SIMPLE IS JUST FINE.

Experiences don't need to be over the top. Keep it simple. Teaching about estimation? Give kids dinner menus, some toy money, and walk around the room taking their orders. How about fractions? Create a museum of fractions and let the students bring in objects for their exhibits. It can even be as simple as letting kids use a microscope. Yeah, kids aren't using microscopes at young ages, and it's terribly sad.

In the chapter "Passion: A Key Ingredient," I told the story of bringing shark teeth into my classroom. We ended up looking at them under a microscope in the science lab. The sad part is that of my 24 fourth-grade students, only 10 knew what a microscope was, and only three of those students had ever used one. What?! Why aren't we giving kids even the simplest experiences? When we went to the lab and examined the teeth, I couldn't get the students to step away from the microscope. We were actually late to Art class that day because the students (and I) were so engaged that we lost track of time. See? Experiences are engaging, impactful, and fun!

## CONNECTED TO OTHERS.

I'm proud to say that I am a National Geographic Certified Educator. While working towards my certification, I was taught that our lessons and experiences should tie us to something bigger: the cultures, the experiences, the histories, the stories, and the traditions of others. Our experiences should open our eyes to see beyond our own schools, cities, states, and more... basically, it should cause us to see beyond ourselves. When I taught my fourth graders one year about how the earth's surface changes because of violent and rapid events (natural disasters) or because of slow and steady changes (weathering and erosion), it was great to give them experiences and let them build demonstrations in the science lab. The kids had a blast and would talk about it the next day. However, that didn't connect us to others, at least not on a deep level.

In order to make this connection and give my students a new perspective, I asked my students to investigate the destruction of the fires in Australia in 2020, which was happening at the time of this experience. Kids started investigating, and I noticed that their first discussions sounded something like this: "Dang, this fire is dangerous. Look, it destroyed the trees and the—wait, what?! It killed how many kangaroos?! That is so sad!" Then I started hearing about ancient cave drawings being destroyed by the fire.

*Me: Why is that catching your attention?*

*Student: Because when people painted on cave walls, it was like their stories, and now they are gone. That's sad.*

*Me: And the animals? Why is that catching your attention?*

*Student: Because I love animals. They are innocent creatures, so this is sad.*

This kid was starting to see beyond the facts. The investigation experience gave him a new set of eyes that allowed him to see through someone's eyes and experience sympathy for them.

We then continued our studies by asking the question: Which state is the most dangerous to live in based on the amount and type of natural disasters in that state? Using an interactive map (I can't remember the specific one, but there are several online), my students were able to graph the frequency and severity of certain natural disasters in the states they were looking into.

The goal wasn't to scare kids away from living in Texas. (Turns out Texas tends to have a high number of natural disasters, according to the students' discoveries when they looked at recent data.) The goal was to give my kids an experience with technology that connected them with fellow Americans in other states. They found out that New Mexico isn't the only state that experiences severe droughts and fires. They thought we had hard winters in New Mexico until they checked out the state of Michigan.

Experiences have to give kids new sets of eyes to see beyond the basics, beyond the obvious. When you plan your experiences, do your best to give kids chances to make big connections to the world around them.

Kids will be way more engaged in an experience than a mere lesson. I had no behavioral issues during that lesson with the shark teeth; the kids were buzzing about it the next day, and it was fun!

---

Teachers, we can't be the teacher from Ferris Bueller's Day Off, lecturing to a room of students whose eyes have glazed over, who have fallen asleep, and are totally zoned out due to boredom! Our kids, at any age and grade level, are begging for us to give them something worth talking about when they get home. They are waiting for us to stop the lecture and put the responsibility of learning back in their hands. No one cares today about the worksheet they did yesterday. They will remember the experiences you give them, and they'll be grateful to you.

*No one cares today about the worksheet they did yesterday.*

The schoolhouse becomes a place where students love to be when the experiences they have there are impacting their lives and developing a love of learning. Experiences aren't just fun; they impact students in huge ways. What type of person will our kids become based on the experiences they get? Will they grow to become forensic scientists? Will they develop a passion for justice and grow to become social activists? What about contractors? Plumbers? Musicians? Which of our students will become business owners? Even if the experience you give impacts just one student, then you have done your job. It's our job to create experiences that will impact their learning and their future. Give them an experience.

**Stop and reflect: What experiences, big or small, do you hope to give kids this year?**

---

*From Noah Valenzuela, (13) - former student of Elijah Carbajal*

An experience that I had was when we were studying gravity and we went outside. We had a couple of objects and we dropped them from far up on the playground equipment and timed how long each object took to fall. Giving me that visual observation helped me understand gravity even more. Through that experience I learned that gravity pulls on each object at the same rate, but since there is a thing called drag each object falls at different speeds. For example, since a feather has more drag than a pen, the feather took longer to fall to the ground than the pen.

The experience made me really interested in physics and intrigued about science in general. I very much liked the concept. I was talking about the concepts with my parents a lot. Plus, since third grade we always talked about it for science time. It also made me curious about how dropping things on different planets would be. Maybe dropping a pen on Jupiter is different from one on Neptune. That is how that experience fostered a love of learning.

My advice for teachers who are trying to create a good experience for students is to make the topic fun. Go outside to demonstrate a point for science or mix two materials together to show a reaction. If it is fun, the students will remember that. They remember that day as a fun day in their year. That is my advice for teachers.

## CHAPTER 15
# POLYPHONIC VOICES

It's no secret that I have a passion for music. I've been playing bass guitar since I was 14 years old and guitar since I was 16 years old. I took piano lessons and music theory classes with my late aunt. I also dabble with drums. Singing? Eh. I can, but I'm not that great. Still, I'm fascinated with talented singers. Probably because it's a weakness of mine.

I took music appreciation in college, and it was in that class that I learned about polyphonic singing. It's when multiple people are singing at the same time, not necessarily harmonizing, though. It's two or more voices having a melody *of their own* while being sung at the same time. If you listen to "Earth Angel" by The Penguins, you can hear multiple voices singing different melodies during the chorus. It's a great song and a great example of polyphonic singing.

There's so much talk of letting students lead the classroom, let their voice be heard, etc. With all that, let us not forget to let *every* voice be heard. We need to work to create the perfect blend of everyone's voice. You see, we teach everyone. The jocks, the nerds, the musicians, the poets, the hunters, the goths, the punks, LGBTQ+ students, multilingual students, students with special needs, the introverts, the extroverts, the kids in drama class, religious/spiritual kids, the kids taking woodshop, the motivated, the unmotivated, Black kids, White kids, everyone! And everyone has a significant voice that needs to be heard.

I hope that you are one of the fortunate ones who get to teach a wide variety of students. Unfortunately, there are teachers who prefer one voice in the classroom; i.e., they only want certain kids in their room. There was a teacher I once knew who, basically, taught the same kids every year: gifted and other high-performing students, most of whom were White. For the most part, she got what she wanted every year: a song with one voice, not polyphonic voices. We must be willing and ready to teach *everyone*.

I'm not about to tell you that the ideas about to be presented are the ultimate solutions to making our classrooms polyphonic, but they will help. Here are just a few ideas.

**Stop and reflect: When it comes to making everyone's voice heard, what successes have you had? What about setbacks?**

## BUILD RELATIONSHIPS WITH YOUR STUDENTS.

As mentioned in the chapter "Let's Talk Relationships," it's important to build positive relationships with students. No teacher is ever going to tell you that teaching is purely academic. We educate the whole child, and teaching beyond academics (social skills, emotional resilience, problem-solving, conflict resolution, etc.) means that we have to have a solid relationship with our students. It's also another way that we make students feel safe in our classes. No one really opens up about who they are and what they're about until a solid relationship is built and connections are made. It will not always come easy, but it will be worth it when your students finally feel comfortable expressing their voice in the classroom.

## CREATE OPPORTUNITIES FOR STUDENTS TO SHARE WHO THEY ARE.

One year, when teaching how to identify the theme of a poem to my fourth graders, I assigned the students to select a song and share it with the class. They had to identify possible themes and any figurative language. They also had to share what the song meant to them. Some of the students got dressed up as the singer of the song they chose. They talked a lot about how the song they chose meant a lot to them because it was related to some of their passions (helping others, sports, determination, and family connections). It was a fantastic opportunity for my students to share a little about who they are as individuals, and I also gained insights into their family life. I've seen other teachers hold fairs in their classrooms, where the students showed collections they had. Everything from Pokémon cards, video games, photo albums, rock collections, and family heirlooms were presented. Again, another great opportunity to show off who they are!

## SHOW STUDENTS THAT YOU ARE PROUD OF WHO THEY ARE.

Showing them, however you can, that you are proud of who they are and celebrate all of their differences will make students feel welcome and safe —safe enough that they too will celebrate their diversity.

## NEVER DISRESPECT ANOTHER STUDENT'S CULTURE.

I taught at a school with a high population of Native American students. Every year, a new batch of fourth graders would come in, and the Native American students would tell me the same thing: that they aren't allowed to look at snakes. So, none of my lessons or examples included pictures of snakes. I was once asked why I would accommodate them in that way, and why it was even such a big deal anyway. I told the person, "It's not a big deal to you, but, according to what they tell me, they are not allowed to look at snakes. It's a big deal to them, so it's a big deal to me. I'm not going to disrespect their culture or their family wishes." You can have a dynamic lesson and still disrespect others' cultures, which is a scary thought. We have to be careful not to disrespect the culture of others. When we do, we silence their voices, and the polyphonic song becomes quieter and quieter.

**Stop and reflect: What ideas do you have that could help create a polyphonic classroom?**

Those simple yet powerful examples go a long way to creating the polyphonic sound of students' voices. It opens doors for students to share who they are, celebrate differences, and take pride in each other. Remember the goal: make school a place that they love. Polyphonic voices are evidence of a school with a healthy culture. Be that teacher that creates an environment where students take pride in themselves and are bold enough to share who they are.

Those polyphonic voices represent something special: a positive classroom culture. It's a culture of respect. It's a culture of celebrating differences and individual identities. It's a culture that students will feel relaxed and comfortable in. It's a culture that students love to be a part of.

# CHAPTER 16

# NOW THAT'S BETTER

W hat do we do when our best isn't enough? There are days, I admit, that no matter how hard I try, I still fall short. It seems that some days, my best isn't good enough. The only option that I have in those moments is to get better—better for ourselves, but also for our students. They need a teacher who is striving for excellence.

In 2019, I attended the Teach Better Conference in Akron, Ohio. It was there I heard this phrase: *Better today than you were yesterday, better tomorrow than you were today.* That's all anyone can really ask for. Be better than you were yesterday. That's all I ask of my students. It's all we should ask of ourselves.

But what does striving to get better look like? How does getting better make school a place that students love to be?

For a teacher, better means different results for our students. Let's imagine a scenario for a minute. Let's say I am a little lazy at lesson planning. What the heck...let's also assume that my lessons suck and are really boring. "Better" doesn't mean that I start being better at planning, but I continue to plan and teach crappy lessons. I can't say that I'm truly getting better, right? Sure, I'm getting more diligent about planning, but I'm not necessarily striving to be better for my kids, especially if my lessons are still boring kids to death. I've got to get better results. "Better" might mean that my kids aren't making every excuse to leave my room. "Better" might mean that my kids are on the edge of their seats, that they are making academic progress, and they are actually learning to apply the content in their world.

Storytime!

During my fifth year of teaching, I dressed as the notorious pirate, Blackbeard. I gave an entire lesson about who he was, his importance to history, and his impact on society. My goal was to teach my students about biographies and to prepare them for their upcoming biography projects. It was successful, but I wanted to be better the next time I did this. The next year, I stepped up my game. About a week before Blackbeard arrived on campus, I began to build up curiosity and suspense.

My students ran up to me with a pouch filled with chocolate gold coins they found by our door. I pretended to send out an email, asking teachers if any of their kids had lost gold coins. I told my students that no one had lost any gold chocolate coins, and then I let my kids eat the chocolate. What came next freaked my students out. That same day, after lunch and after they devoured the chocolate, another mysterious pouch was waiting for my students. Inside was a note:

*Give back me gold coins or suffer my wrath! Consider this your only warning.*
                                                                                *-Blackbeard*

As if a note was enough to freak them out, out of the bag was another artifact. I pulled it out and slowly and carefully unfolded Blackbeard's pirate flag!

So, Blackbeard was ready to make an appearance, right? Not without a little more added suspense. A couple of days later, a bandana with a jolly roger was found tied to our classroom door handle. The next day "someone" mysteriously drew a pirate skull on the whiteboard. I also asked Tracey Taylor (who I worked with at the time) for some help. As my kids walked by her room, they saw her flipping a gold pirate coin that she had! They just about lost it!

So, you can imagine how they freaked out when Blackbeard picked them up from the cafeteria that day! Hanging over our door, Blackbeard's flag!

I taught about Blackbeard that day and taught what should be included in a biography report, but this time it was better!

But I wasn't done there. I drew a black spot on my hand and wrapped my hand with the pirate bandanna. When they asked why I did this, I fibbed a short story that my pirate crew and I robbed a ship with cursed gold. Because it was cursed, I was marked with the horrific black spot. I also explained that I began getting rid of the gold coins so that the curse would pass to another person who possessed the coins...then they made the connection: Tracey Taylor was walking around flipping a gold coin! Oh, no!

*"Blackbeard, how could you do that to our art teacher?!"*

*"Hey, I'm a pirate! What did you expect?"*

They really got concerned when their art teacher showed up with a black spot on her hand the next day!

---

Better! I could have easily done things the same as I did the year before, but why? Because it's comfortable? Because it's easy? Those are reasons why some aren't striving to be better. But that's not the mentality we should have if we are trying to make our schools a place that students love. We should have a mentality that strives to be better for our kids.

So are we trying to be better? Are we reading books that will help us better our practice? Are we connecting to teachers at our school or over social media? When was the last time we attended a teaching conference? What are we doing to be better?

**Stop and reflect: What was the last educational book you read (besides this one)? How did it impact you?**

Don't beat yourself up if you have setbacks. We all do. We are human, and sometimes we are just off our game. It happens to all of us. The goal is to be better, not perfect. If we can look in the mirror and say that we messed up, make a plan to be better, and execute it the next day, then we are on the right path. But never be too hard on yourself. We are learning, just like our students.

What have you done lately to be better for your students, your staff, your family, or yourself? Make a plan, stick with it, and watch yourself become better.

_____

*From Chad Ostrowski, M.S. Ed - Author of "Teach Better" / CEO - Teach Better Team*

Be better today than you were yesterday and better tomorrow than you were today. This has been the philosophy of the TEACH BETTER Team since its inception. Sometimes better means focusing on relationships, sometimes it means more purposefully planning or increasing engagement in your classroom. Sometimes "Better" can even mean taking care of yourself. The point of this mantra is not to funnel educators or anyone into a specific better but to instill a mindset of continuous improvement. Better is a call, a driving force, a motivational commitment to focus on what you can improve every single day for the learners in your classroom.

Not every day is going to be perfect and in reality, sometimes entire school years are going to feel like you're drowning. If we are striving for perfection or to fix everything at once, the task and the process becomes overwhelming and impossible.

If we just focus on small steps, individual pieces of ourselves, our instruction, or how we interact with students or our teaching, we can confidently say that we are "Better" today than we were the day before. The best thing about this is that it's amazing what all of those small steps can accomplish and the monumental changes and improvements they can have on a student, teacher, school, or district. Better never stops, it's never finished, and it's a process that doesn't end, but its pursuit can allow you to continually grow and thrive as an educator.

This is one of the most honorable characteristics of educators, that we never "settle" for what was, and are always focused on what can be. We aren't satisfied with 99% of our students learning because it's that last 1% we want to continue to reach. As educators, "Better" is what we do, "Better" is who we are, "Better" represents all that we can become and our continuous pursuit of the impossible but with the constant successes and growth that allow us to thrive.

## CHAPTER 17
# DEAR ADMINISTRATION

Dear Administration,
    I hope, so far, that you are enjoying this book. I hope that you are learning a lot. Maybe, you are doing a book study with your staff, and together you are making changes and identifying what strengths you have that contribute to making school a place that students love.

I love you, administrators. I know that your job is stressful. Trust me, I applaud you for your work. I sure as heck don't want to do it. You have a demanding job. You have to work with teachers, parents, and students. You have to think about safety, budgeting, discipline, observations, data analysis, and much more. You have a lot on your plate, and I want you to understand that I truly appreciate you for the work you do. Please don't read this as hate mail, and please understand that I'm not referring to every administrator or school.

However, I have some concerns, my first being this: why do *some* administrators insist on taking recess away from kids? Trust me, I wish that the favorite thing about school was being in the science lab, or the research projects that classes are doing, but, still, so many students tell fellow teachers and me that the favorite part of their day is recess. I'm sure that you've heard of and maybe even read about the studies that have shown that recess is beneficial and can actually improve learning. According to the CDC, recess is important and benefits students by:

- Increasing their level of physical activity.
- Improving their memory, attention, and concentration.
- Helping them stay on-task in the classroom.
- Reducing disruptive behavior in the classroom.
- Improving their social and emotional development (e.g., learning how to share and negotiate). (*Recess* 2019)

That 10-minute break of "unstructured" time when kids can run, jump, shoot hoops, swing, or just sit and laugh with a friend can be just the thing to reset a kid's brain and make them ready to go learn again. Yet, it's still a common disciplinary practice of administration and teachers to take recess away for the day. Why?

Think about it: we expect students to stay in class, even really engaging classes, for close to six hours a day, but they can't have a recess for 10 minutes because they forgot to bring their agenda to school? Kids need a break. Even older students in middle and high school need a break of some sort. I mean, don't we take breaks to eat lunch, go to the bathroom, get some water, etc.? When a student loses recess (remember, we're talking 10 minutes out of a six-hour day), this is the message they receive: *fun, free time, and relationships are not as important as we claim that they are.* Please, don't take away recess as a form of punishment. I get that some behavior problems can occur on the playground. Kids can find themselves getting into trouble for lots of reasons, but there has to be another solution. One year, at a school I worked at, the principal told us *not to take away recess as a form of punishment.* (A couple of teachers and I actually started clapping at that moment. Preeeeeach!) What we began to do for students who need some redirection (not a punishment) is teach the behavior we want to see. Instead of making them sit out for the entire recess, a teacher might pull them aside for a quick couple of minutes to have that needed conversation about expectations. Once an understanding and an agreement is met, the student is sent back on their way to play. Some teachers would do this while walking with the student, so that the student still gets some kind of movement. There were rarely any issues with this approach. What I'm trying to say is, there are other solutions besides taking away recess.

I'm just going to say it: *writing should never be used as a form of punishment.* You see, even if it's writing apology letters, it's still being used as a form of punishment, and it hurts kids' love of writing. It tells them that writing is to be used as punishment. It's no wonder kids hate writing. They view it as a punishment, so when your teachers ask them to write, they think, because they have been conditioned to do so, that they are being punished. Writing should be fun! It should be a challenge that students are eager to tackle, but they often see it as torture. It's because some administrators have deemed it appropriate to make kids write apology letters and "caught being good" notes to students when they get in trouble. Apology notes should be sincere, not demanded. "Caught being good" notes should be used to reinforce positive behavior, not to make amends after kids have been in trouble for fighting with each other. We have future authors, storytellers, and researchers in our class who are eager to write. That is until they are forced to write "I will not talk back" 100 times. Administration, don't punish kids by making them write, and don't allow your teachers to use writing as punishment either.

Admin, there will be times when students are in serious violation of school rules. I ask that you do what is best for the student. Discipline is important, but so is restoration. I won't tell you what to do in situations when students are in serious violation of school rules. I can, however, speak from my experience and from the stories I've heard about how important setting up restorative circles and restorative conversations are. Remember, we are educators. We can use these moments to *teach* students about right and wrong, good and bad, how to solve problems in a healthy way, and how to reflect on their words and actions. Take the right action, and I'm not necessarily talking about suspensions. Admin, start by providing professional development so that your teachers have a solid understanding of restorative practices and help to implement this practice across your entire school.

*Are you still reading? Do you still love me? Good. Let's continue.*

Please don't forget that we teach students of families struggling with poverty. I've taught in suburban areas where families are doing their best to make ends meet. I've taught kids who pack snacks from the school lunch so that they have something to eat when they get home. I have taught kids who are living out of their family vehicle. When America and the world got hit hard by the COVID-19 pandemic, so many eyes were opened up to the fact that the "haves and the have nots" are real. The public really began to see everything that schools do for students. During that time, a lot of schools still set high expectations for their students, but they made sure that ALL students had the right tools to meet those expectations. Teachers dropped off supplies for students who didn't have any at home. They made packets for students who didn't have access to the internet. Administrators were leading with equity in mind because they were aware that not every student's situation is bright and happy. I want to encourage you to continue to do this, administrators, to lead with equity, and continue to do what you can to make sure that every student has what they need to be successful.

Next, continue to lean on your teachers. Listen to and consider their ideas and their input. Remember that they are experts. They may not be blogging, speaking at conferences, leading professional development, or writing books, but they are still experts. They deserve to be trusted, respected, and heard. There are teachers that may not fit inside a box, which is good because they can offer a new perspective on a situation you're facing. Don't write them off because they are outsiders. There are brand new teachers on your campus who have fresh ideas, and there are veteran teachers who have experience. The specials teachers, the ones who are often looked at as "nice-ities, not necessities" (something I was literally told by another teacher once), the ones some refer to as "just the art teacher" or "just the P.E. coach," are experts in their field and deserve to be respected and heard. Be wary of placing demands on them that are unrealistic and overburdensome, or explaining your reasoning with the phrase, "Because I said so." (I've literally been told that by an administrator, by the way.) Instead, feed them with quality professional development. Coach them. Appreciate them and the work that they do. Answer their questions. Listen to their concerns. Discuss the possibility of rolling out a new idea from them. Remember, school needs to be a place that teachers love too!

Administrators, your teachers, school staff members, and students have trauma. Some of them are coping through unhealthy means. I know because I was that teacher, riddled with anxiety, depression, and trauma. I wasn't healthy, and I didn't have the courage to tell anyone what I was dealing with. By the grace of God, I eventually found healthy ways to cope and move past some of the ugliness, including some unhealthy and dangerous coping methods. Some teachers haven't found healthy ways to cope. Some are not mentally healthy and are struggling so much inside with no one to talk to. Some students—yes, the students in our schools— are in the same place. Admin, please, Please, PLEASE, take the mental health of everyone—yourself, teachers, staff, and students—seriously. Please, don't tell us to practice self-care after you just tripled our workload. Ask us how we honestly feel. Be honest with us; you are human, after all, and have your own stresses. I don't pretend that all the stress of school and its side effects falls only on the teachers. There will never be any judgment from me if you ever need to talk it out. Create an environment that normalizes and promotes a healthy mental state for all individuals. I will forever be thankful for one of my former principals, Natalie Martinez, who listened to me and gave me the time and space to calm down during an intense panic attack. Principals, be that person for your teachers! And for goodness sake, stop giving perfect attendance awards to teachers! Make mental health days a thing!

Lastly, remember to have fun. School should be a place that you love too. I get excited to see principals outside greeting kids in the pickup line or at the bus line. I love to see administrators out at recess with the kids, playing tetherball or kickball. Do you know who gets excited even more? The kids! I also think that those principals are truly enjoying themselves. Yes, you have a serious job to do, but you also need to take time to do some- thing fun at work. Kids shouldn't see teachers as the fun parent while viewing you as the strict, no-fun parent. School should be a place that everyone—students, teachers, and administrators—loves.

I love you, administrators. You are NOT the enemy. We are not on different teams. This place called school becomes the most enjoyable, comfortable, and safe environment when we ALL work together to make it that. You are valuable and important, and the success of a school requires a strong administrator, such as yourself. Don't ever take that lightly.

Sincerely,
A teacher who loves you

**PS: Teachers, give a shoutout to one of your administrators via social media, a text message, or a handwritten note. Make it sincere and personal. Administrators, now do the same for one of your teachers.**

---

*From Michael Earnshaw, Husband, Father, Principal, Co-Host of Punk Rock Classrooms Podcast, and Author of The EduCultureCookbook: Recipes & Dishes to Positively Transform Classroom & School Culture (@MikeREarnshaw / @PunkClassrooms)*

### Breaking the Mold

While I am proud to say I am not one of the administrators that Elijah is pleading to, I am still saddened because I know that there are so many in the field of education doing *exactly* what he is stating we should not, nor cannot do. Elijah's chapter has hit me directly in the heart, not so much because I am the opposite of the administrators he is trying to reach, but because I am a father of a child with severe ADHD and anxiety.

Recess should never be taken away from students. Period. I'm not going to rehash the reasons why as Elijah has already explained it better than I ever could. But let me ask you this. As an educator, whether you are a classroom teacher, specialist, paraprofessional, or whatever, what emotions do you experience when your plan time gets cut short, or your lunch? I've seen it firsthand when I needed to inform staff that we don't have a sub for their students' Specials class, and they will not have the much-needed thirty-five-minute plan time for the day. I don't need to reenact or narrate that conversation and observation of the staff member's body language; we've all experienced it. If you value your own personal "brain break" time, why wouldn't we value and honor those of our students? They need that "down time" just as much, if not more than we do.

My son has extreme ADHD. He needs to run, to move, to spin, to stand. He has had teachers in his past that would explain how he misbehaves and is off-task when they require him to sit quietly in his seat. Even worse, when his recess has been taken from him as punishment, for his non-compliance to sit quietly, the rest of his day is thrown off. I never understood their rationale or surprise at this. His ADHD is documented. He has multiple accommodations listed, so what did they expect? Many years ago, I informed our staff that no recess would be taken away from any student. I was first greeted with resistance, with many believing this was the only way to "get through" to a child. By providing research and techniques on various restorative practices and the benefits of recess, our staff was quick to see firsthand the benefits it brought. Fewer behavior problems. More student focus and engagement. Some staff even began incorporating more micro-recess breaks throughout the day! Bottom line, we all need "brain breaks," staff, and students of every level.

Speaking of movement, principals, why are your faculty meetings typically you reading bullet points to your staff, most of which can be sent in an email? Faculty meetings are traditionally held after teachers have spent an exhausting day empowering our students. The last thing they want is to listen to you drone on for an hour. We expect them to bring engagement and various learning styles to our students, so why would you do any different for them? Get up, get moving. Take your faculty meetings outside. Break into groups. Play games. Laugh together. And believe it or not, these can all be accomplished while still analyzing data and problem-solving issues your school may be facing! Don't believe me? Well, shameless plug, you knew it was coming, then pick up my book, *The EduCulture-Cookbook: Recipes and Dishes to Positively Transform Classroom and School Culture,* where I share many amazing activities our staff has completed! Don't worry teachers, everything I have done can be done with students.

Self-care has become so cliche, but it is so powerful. If administrators are not modeling and partaking in self-care themselves, they should not be telling their staff to. Administrators, we must walk the talk and let our actions show what we say. I encourage our staff to take care of themselves, and I share with them how I find time in my busy schedule of being a father, husband, leader, and friend. My alarm goes off at 5:00 am. I chug a coffee and am then running miles, pedaling away on our Peloton, or my favorite, lifting some heavy weights. This is my time, and I am not doing my best for myself, my family, our staff, or students if I skip "me time." You may need to make sacrifices, get up earlier, go to bed later, but trust me, the benefits outweigh what you're giving up. Also, my email is "asleep" at 5:00 pm each day and throughout the weekend. I know how important family time is, so I model disconnecting from "the job" each day. Guess what? Our school is still running as smoothly as ever without after-hours emails.

Lastly, suspensions. We rarely suspend students from school. Students need to be IN school, not away. It's our responsibility to teach students appropriate choices and coping skills. How are we going to accomplish that while they are sitting at home? Find ways to reach, connect, and teach kids while they are with you. Suspensions do not solve any issues; they just prolong them and give students an escape.

Take time for yourself, and you will be there for those you serve. Invest in people; build positive and trusting relationships, and you will be able to move mountains together and empower our students to know they can change the world.

# CHAPTER 18
# THE IMPORTANCE OF FAILING

I love to share my successes because I believe that success produces confidence. When I finish running a new distance, I know that I can do that again. Success builds confidence. That's why I love to share my successes and see the successes of my friends and family. What's hard for me to show are my failures and weaknesses. It's easy to show off the days that are good, and it's easier to stay quiet on the days that are bad. Now, I will say that as I have matured as an individual and as a teacher, I have become more comfortable admitting my faults and any shortcomings I have, but it can still be intimidating. Displaying your failures flies in the face of what society tells us we should be: perfect all the time.

I think that social media has made it very difficult for us to be honest with those we interact with and even with ourselves. I think our social media feeds are often filled with a lot of content that makes us think that things are always great for certain people. They always have the greatest-this or the latest-that. Every picture of your friend reminds you of how smokin' hot she is *every day* and how average you always seem. Every post is another success of a friend, making you feel like a failure.

You might feel like a failure, but that's okay, because your smokin' hot friend eventually has to take her make-up off and reveal the blemishes. Your other friend is actually only showing off his highlight reel, and behind every highlight reel, there is a blooper reel, and some of them are downright cringe-worthy. In other words, no one is perfect, and everyone fails. Jennie Magiera's ISTE keynote from 2017 backs this point up. She cites evidence that found that Americans who use social media tend to exaggerate or even lie about how they feel, including claims from one source (Stephens-Davidowitz, *Don't Let Facebook Make You Miserable,* 2017) that what we post on Facebook and what we search for on Google tend to contradict each other (*Setting Free the Untold Stories in Education: Jennie Magiera @ ISTE* 2017). (Observe the following photo of Seth Stephens-Davidowitz's findings during his research about what people actually post on Facebook and search on Google.)

## "I always..."

| | |
|---|---|
| *am on vacation* | feel tired |
| *am having brunch* | have to pee |
| *am taking selfies* | have diarrhea |
| *am living #bestlifeever* | am bloated |

Seth Stephens-Davidowitz, NYT 2017

(Caption: Slide from Magiera, 2017, ISTE Keynote)

I'm no expert, but it seems like a lot of people are #fakehappy, showing off their #bestlifeever, all while they are trying to figure out this thing called #therealworld, just like all of us.

Searching for perfection is dangerous because the end result is always disappointment. Perfection is never attainable, so disappointment will always be present.

*Wait, Elijah, what does this have to do with making school a place that students love?*

I'm glad you asked.

## FAIL THE RIGHT WAY.

Everyone is going to fail...everyone. You, me, them, and all of us again. So I think it's important to model how to fail. We need to be teaching our students how to fail the right way. There's a lot of growth-mindset-type quotes out there about failure, but they basically all say this: *You only fail if you quit.* If you stop trying, you have failed. Can you imagine how much our students would grow if we modeled this to them daily? You see, we have to fail, but only with the right mindset. A failure only leads to success when we stop, reflect, plan, and execute.

Storytime!

I was excited to get started with a math lesson: fraction addition and subtraction and fraction equivalence. My kids played a game the day before that they were so pumped up about that they asked to play it today. The kids were amped this morning and excited to get started. Like, *really* excited. When I said, "We're going to play that same game we played yesterday," all chaos erupted. Kids started moving before some other necessary directions were given. The volume in the room was at 100. Some kids forgot which group they were in, and so they began wandering around the room chatting with friends. Others were frustrated that no one was giving them the materials they needed.

*A failure only leads to success when we stop, reflect, plan, and execute.*

I wish I could tell you that I respectfully got their attention, calmly asked the kids to return to their seats, and clearly gave directions and expectations. But, this is a story of my failure. It became, for a moment, like a game of Teacher-Whack-a-Mole, trying my best to redirect each kid one at a time. You know how that game goes...

"No, you go there."

"Hey, wait. That's not your group!"

"Why are you walking around doing nothing?!"

"Why are you shouting?!"

"EVERYONE STOP!"

"I'm about to lose it with you all! Get it together now!"

I realized, too late, that I wasn't the calm one in the room. I realized that I was also shouting. I was the one who was adding to their chaos. Sure, they didn't listen to all my directions, and yes, they didn't bother to ask me for clarification. Come on, though. I'm the teacher who is supposed to remain calm in the chaos. I'm the one who is supposed to redirect students calmly. I'm the one who is supposed to respectfully speak with students, not scream back at them.

Epic.

Fail.

**Stop and reflect: Have you failed lately? What lessons did it teach you?**

*Failure is only an end if we allow it to be.*

The story's not over yet. My own loud voice made me stop, cringe inside, and calmly say, "I'm sorry. Please go back to your seats." I walked to the front of the room. All my students had that worried and anxious look on their faces. As calmly as I could, I said, "I'm sorry. That was crazy, huh? I was frustrated because no one listened to directions, but in my frustration, I made you frustrated, huh? I apologize. Please forgive me. Let's try this again." This time, I gave my directions, students listened, and then we started our activities. The atmosphere felt different. The students were more focused, and everyone was a lot calmer.

I learned something. Failure is only an end if we allow it to be. I could've hung my head after I realized I had failed. I could've let that setback beat me down the rest of the day. I could've also blamed the students, read them the riot act, and then complained about it to my peers. Instead, I decided to breathe, reset, and analyze the situation. It was quick. I identified the problem (my own actions), made a corrective decision, and carried out the plan. I'm happy to say that the rest of the math period went very well. I can't imagine how it would've gone if I kept yelling at my students or beating myself up for my shortcomings. Or both.

I had to model failure and how to bounce back from a failure. A lot of teachers might not have looked at the screaming I did as a failure because the kids erupted into chaos like Mount Vesuvius first. I did, though. Screaming is not classroom management. It's a last-ditch effort to gain control. A teacher who is in control of their classroom doesn't need to yell at their students. I like to think that I have decent classroom management. It's obviously not perfect because I lost my cool with those kids like a penguin in the desert. To some students, that is normal. My students know that I rarely, if ever, yell. I'm not sure why my frustration level was so low that day, but it was, and it shouldn't have been.

The first thing I had to model was admission upon realization. I've learned that when I fail, I need to admit to it for the purpose of learning from it as soon as I realize it. When I know I've wronged someone or possibly offended someone, I do my best to make things right, and it starts with apologizing or admitting to a failure or shortcoming. I told my students, "In my frustration, I made you frustrated, huh?" That was me owning up to a failure of mine. Teachers, you have to be okay with apologizing to your students when you are in the wrong. We model for our students, whether we know it or not. If we model humility, they will follow in your footsteps because you made it okay to be vulnerable enough to say, "I failed."

The next thing this does is bust the perfect teacher myth. Every year I always hear a couple of my students say something to the effect of, "Mr. C. will know that because he is the teacher, he just knows everything." Nope. Not everything. Not even close. At that moment, I didn't know, or at least recognize, my need for patience and to fall back on what I know are best practices for classroom management. I also broke part of our classroom vision. In our classroom vision, the students said they wanted *less shouting and yelling*. So, no, I'm far from perfect. No one is, and our students need to know this if they are going to leave school with a realistic view of life, not the social media view of life.

I needed to model a second chance. "Please forgive me. Let's try this again." If you are truly okay with your students taking risks and failing, you have to be okay with giving them a second chance. Academically, this could mean letting students complete retakes as they work towards mastery. It could look like giving your student a second chance at learning how to use tools in the science lab appropriately instead of banning him from ever using them again. There are no perfect schools, but there are lots of schools with second chances, and I think second chances are beautiful.

**Stop and reflect: What second chances have you given your students that have enhanced their learning experience?**

## THE IMPORTANCE OF FAILURE.

We've already established that no one is perfect, including our students. They are going to fail. Get used to that. Maybe not at everything or every day, but yes, even your "smartest" student is going to fail at something this year, or at least they should. See, I believe failures and struggles produce strength when they are met with hard work, dedication, and the right mindset. When we fail, we should actually look at it as an opportunity to solve a problem, not as a final declaration of who we are. Failure allows us to use critical thinking skills to solve problems and turn a failure into success. If you aren't failing, then you simply are not being challenged and without a challenge to overcome, you will never have true and continued success. So with this view, I would argue that if we don't allow our students to fail then we are doing them a disservice.

*When we fail, we should actually look at it as an opportunity to solve a problem.*

I'm not married to the word "rigor," but is the work rigorous enough that it will challenge students to think critically, reflect personally, or apply multiple skills? If our students are expected to do big things, our activities and work in the classroom should be rigorous. Rigorous work, however, is challenging and might result in failure from your students. It's in these moments I remember what an assistant principal told me once about letting kids catch themselves when they are wrong. If we rush in to save and correct students when they are wrong, then they will never experience the failure and the process of reflection and correction. When we don't let kids fail, when we constantly correct them ourselves with no room for self-reflection, we do our students a disservice. They need to experience failure.

*Okay, Elijah. I'm lost. I thought school was supposed to be a place students love. How can that be when you expect them to experience failure?*

I firmly believe that what the assistant principal said about allowing kids to catch themselves when they fail is an overlooked best practice in education. When I started applying her feedback to my teaching, I started hearing a lot more, "Wait...oooooooh, now I get it, Mr. C." (A phrase I love to hear, by the way!) I don't hear kids say that when I say, "No, that's not the answer. Here let me help." What I'm trying to say is that failure and the right approach to failure produce deeper understanding. It means that learning is enhanced. When kids learn, they are excited about school. Enhanced student learning through failure, in a sense, allows schools to become a place they love! Not that they will love failure. Failure kind of sucks when it's happening in front of us. It won't always be pretty. But they will love the process of learning, which includes failure. They will love the teachers that modeled how to fail correctly. They will love the teachers that made failure okay and normal and safe. They will love the teachers that taught them the importance of failing and helped them turn their failures into successes!

**Stop and reflect: What opportunities for growth have you found as a result of a failure?**

# CONCLUSION: YOU JUST NEVER KNOW

My wife, Tracey Taylor, is an amazing art teacher. She's an extremely talented artist. Every time she paints, she makes magic on a canvas. Her work is truly captivating. (Tracey, you are my favorite artist!)

When she paints, sometimes I will DJ for her. I try to keep the variety of music wide, but every now and then, I just get hung up on a band. One night it was The Beatles. We were both listening intently that night to the music and lyrics of songs like "I Am the Walrus," "Across the Universe," "Get Back," "Carry That Weight," "I Will," and one of her all-time favorite Beatles songs, "Come Together."

I started to really think about what music is: a collection of pitches played together to create a brand new sound. When certain notes are played together, they make a chord. When more chords are added together and played in a certain pattern, it creates a rhythm. When a sequence of notes are played, it creates a melody. When lyrics are added to the melody, it becomes the song we all sing. Sing that over the collection of chords played, and you have a song.

It was mind-blowing to continue thinking that all of what music is has such a tremendous impact on the mind, the emotions, and even the physical feelings of a person. Music has helped people get through some of the darkest times. A lot of times, music has memories attached to them. Music gave me hope when I had none. It made me feel like someone else understood what I was going through, like someone finally gets me.

"Hey Jude" came on next. "Hey Jude" is about hope in dark times. I'm sure that many people have found encouragement in that song. A question popped into my mind: *Did Paul McCartney and John Lennon have any idea that this song, or any of their songs for that matter, would change someone's life? Did The Beatles ever think that the music they were writing would change the world?*

The answer is probably "no." They may have dreamed about their potential, about the impact that their music and their lives would have on millions of people, but I'd almost bet that when they picked up a pen to write lyrics or they sat down to record a song, that there was a little bit of uncertainty. Artists, you see, are gamblers. The Beatles gambled with every song they wrote. Will it be a hit or a flop? Will it impact countless people, inspire them, help them through dark times? Will this song meet its fate along with the list of countless songs that are never remembered?

Did they know? Did they have any idea how much of an impact they were making with their music? I don't think they did. I don't think anyone truly knows what the aftermath of their actions and words will be.

I didn't comprehend just how severe the consequences of some of my past actions would be. I didn't know that some of my words would spit venom at the people they were directed to. I would never have said or done certain things if I knew just how much they would hurt people. However, I also didn't know just how important it was for me to do things like earning my National Geographic Educator Certification until it changed how I taught. I didn't know that getting on Twitter would connect me with some of the most creative and innovative educators I've ever known.

You just never know.

As I wrap up my thoughts in this book—thank you for reading this, by the way!—I want to encourage you with those words. You just never know how what you say or do is going to change a kid's life. For better or worse, we impact students. Even if they look back on their life and say that you made no impact, you did. Whether the student admits it or not, there is an impact that you make on them, for better or worse.

So what does this mean for us as educators? It means that we need to bring our A-Game. That we need to shut up and teach. That we need to search for ways to transform a lesson into an experience. It's a call to make school and the students in your school safe. It's a call to make sure that students are having fun, that school isn't a place that they dread, but a place that they love. We should be striving to make the most positive impact on a child's life. We shouldn't be squandering opportunities to go to a student's wrestling match or their track meet, knowing that it could be a game changer for that student, or calling a parent to ask about how their game went. You just never know how your words will affect your students, so watch what you say and be quick to apologize when you are out of line.

I want to leave you with encouragement. Whatever you have been hoping to do with your students, do it! Do it big, too! Don't settle for okay or good enough. Don't settle for doing something easy over something great! Don't settle for worksheets when you students are dying to take over the learning themselves with projects, songs, dances, reenactments, or other methods. Strive for excellence, not mediocrity. Bring your passion into the classroom. Bring their passion into the classroom. Help them become the best version of themselves. Don't impress them; inspire them!

You just never know how you will impact students. They are yours for an entire school year. That's nine months, five days a week, and 6-7 hours a day. That's more than enough time to change a life, to inspire students, and foster a love of learning.

You have everything it takes to be creative, and even if you don't believe in yourself, I bet there is at least one teacher on your campus that believes in you. And I believe in you. Connect with me if you haven't already (Twitter and Instagram: @carbaeli, Facebook: Elijah Carbajal) and let's help each other grow. There are others who believe in you, and their belief in your abilities and their trust in you can make all the difference in the world: *it's the students inside your classroom.*

Do everything you are able to do to make school a place that students love.

# ACKNOWLEDGMENTS

First and foremost, I want to thank Jesus Christ for blessing me with more than I can imagine. You are truly good to those who love you. You saved my soul, and kept me alive when death was lurking. Thank you, Jesus.

Tracey Taylor. Who would've guessed, right? The road of life has given both of us some unexpected and painful turns, but they all led us to each other. I'm happy for that year when we read and bonded over *Kids Deserve It*. Little did I know that you would be the mentor teacher I had needed all along. Very little did I know that, down the road, you would become so much more to me than a mentor. You are my courage when I have none. You are my compass when I'm lost. You are the candlelight and the wildfire. You are my favorite. I love you, T.

Dad, thank you for imparting wisdom to me. I hope that I have brought honor to our family name, and I pray that you are as proud of me as I am of you. Your commitment to our family is something I will always be thankful for. I love you.

Momma, I've been told that I lead and manage my classes with calmness, and I'm convinced that I get my calm teaching demeanor from you (which is a good thing). Your love and dedication to raising and teaching me and the siblings is something I will always be grateful for. I love you.

Ricky, Jonah, Stephen, Michael, and Francesca, you are my best friends, and I can't imagine life without any of you. I'm proud to call you my siblings, and I'm proud of the lives you have built, the families you have started, and the love you have for our family. I love you all.

There are some educators that I would like to mention by name because of the way they have, personally or through their work, challenged and encouraged me to grow into the teacher I am today. So, in no particular order...Becky Schnekser, Taylor Armstrong, Mike Earnshaw, Josh Buckley, Chad Ostrowski, Deanna Barela, Jessica LaCour, Dr. Dave Schmittou, Dr. Rick Jetter, Charles Williams, Santiago Meza, Jessica Loffredo, Melisa Hayes, Tara Desiderio, Heidi Dudley, Adrienne Jaramillo, Dennis Mathew, Mark Henry, Chey Cheney, Pav Wander, Adam Welcome, Todd Nesloney, and Dave Burgess. Big love to everyone from the Teach Better family. Thank you.

Last but definitely not least, everyone at EduMatch Publishing, especially Sarah Thomas and Mandy Froelich. Musicians and singers are only as good as their producers. Thank you for being my Dr. Dre and Rick Rubin. You all have accepted me into the EduMatch family with open arms. This book is my heart, so thank you for helping to make this come to life.

# NOTES

## FROM THE CHAPTER "THE UNKNOWN"

Ostrowski, C., Jargas, J., Hughart, R., & Ott, T. (2019). *Teach Better*. Dave Burgess Consulting Inc.

"The Grid Method - Free Online Course." *RSS*, www.teachbetteracademy.com/p/the-grid-method-free-online-course.

## FROM THE CHAPTER "THE ENGAGED TEACHER"

Will, M. (2021, September 16). Teachers Are Not OK, Even Though We Need Them to Be. Education Week. Retrieved October 30, 2021, from https://www.edweek.org/teaching-learning/teachers-are-not-ok-even-though-we-need-them-to-be/2021/09.

Leichtman, K. (2021, May 7). *How to Fight Burnout.*
Edutopia. Retrieved October 3, 2021, from
https://www.edutopia.org/article/how-fight-
burnout.

## FROM THE CHAPTER "PASSION: A KEY INGREDIENT"

"Rigor Noun - DEFINITION, PICTURES, Pronunciation and Usage Notes: Oxford ADVANCED American Dictionary at
Oxfordlearnersdictionaries.com." *Rigor Noun -
Definition, Pictures, Pronunciation and Usage
Notes | Oxford Advanced American Dictionary at
OxfordLearnersDictionaries.com*, www.ox-
fordlearnersdictionaries.com/us/definition/amer-
ican_english/rigor.

Malmquist, A. (2021, September 21). *How Passionate
Teaching Can Inspire Students.* Today's Learner.
Retrieved September 26, 2021, from https://to-
dayslearner.cengage.com/how-passionate-teach-
ing-can-inspire-students/.

Johnson, J., Rochkind, J., Ott, A. N., & DuPont, S.
(2009). With Their Whole Lives Ahead of Them.
San Francisco: Public Agenda.

## FROM THE CHAPTER "KEEP IT FRESH"

*Seesaw | Where Learning Happens.* Seesaw. (n.d.).
https://web.seesaw.me/.

Petty, B. (2020). *Create.* Dave Burgess Consulting Inc.

McKinney, G., & Rondot, Z. (2021). Learning from Experts. In *The Expert Effect* (pp. 34–35). Essay, EduMatch.

## FROM THE CHAPTER "SHUT UP AND TEACH"

Froehlich, M. (n.d.). *Education: Mandy FROEHLICH and Divergent edu.* Mandy Froehlich. https://www.mandyfroehlich.com/.

Cherry, K. (2021, February 1). *Why Toxic Positivity Can Be So Harmful.* Verywell Mind. Retrieved October 7, 2021, from https://www.verywell-mind.com/what-is-toxic-positivity-5093958.

## FROM THE CHAPTER "A SAFE PLACE TO BE"

Peck, B. (2019, November 11). *What You Should Know Before Sharing This 'Inspirational' Trauma Meme.* The Mighty. Retrieved September 18, 2021, from https://themighty.com/2019/11/trauma-is-not-your-fault-period/.

Sarah Lewis, P. D. (2020, October 16). *Achluophobia (fear of the dark): Causes, symptoms & treatments.* Healthgrades. Retrieved September 12, 2021, from https://www.healthgrades.com/right-care/anxi-ety-disorders/achluophobia-fear-of-the-dark

## FROM THE CHAPTER "BE THE MARIGOLD"

Seleshanko, Kristina. "Good Flowers to Plant with
Marigolds." *Hunker*, www.hunker.-
com/12593563/good-flowers-to-plant-with-
marigolds.

## FROM THE CHAPTER "DEAR ADMINISTRATION"

Centers for Disease Control and Prevention. (2019,
May 29). *Recess*. Centers for Disease Control and
Prevention. Retrieved September 18, 2021, from
https://www.cdc.gov/healthyschools/physicalac-
tivity/recess.htm.

## FROM THE CHAPTER "THE IMPORTANCE OF FAILING"

Magiera, J. (2017, November 21). Setting Free the
Untold Stories in Education: Jennie Magiera @
ISTE. YouTube. Retrieved September 26, 2021,
from https://youtu.be/MgIAh4_1EvE?t=1475.

Stephens-davidowitz, S. (2017, May 6). *Don't Let Facebook Make You Miserable*. The New York Times.
Retrieved September 26, 2021, from
https://www.nytimes.com/2017/05/06/opin-
ion/sunday/dont-let-facebook-make-you-miser-
able.html.

# ABOUT THE AUTHOR

Elijah is a teacher, like his mom, uncle, and grandparents before him. He has been teaching in the state of New Mexico since 2014, currently working in the Albuquerque Public School District. Elijah enjoys blogging and podcasting about all things education. He strives to make school a place that students love to be at by creating fun, safe, and engaging experiences and environments for all students. By challenging the norms of what education should look, act, and feel like, Elijah has created exciting opportunities for authentic learning to take place. Outside of the classroom, he can be found hanging out with his wife Tracey, running, listening to or creating music, reading, podcasting, writing poetry, or relaxing with his cat, Nala.

Connect with Elijah for speaking engagements and professional development opportunities.

- Twitter and Instagram: @carbaeli
- Facebook: Elijah Carbajal
- Hashtags: #ShutUpAndTeach, #APlaceTheyLoveBook
- Email: shutupandteachedu@gmail.com
- Podcast: The Shut Up and Teach Podcast

Eden Match

PUBLISHING

Made in the USA
Monee, IL
22 March 2024

54833396R00089